TODAY'S INSPIRED *Young* LATINA

VOLUME IV

DREAMS AND ASPIRATIONS FROM THE NEXT GENERATION

Jacqueline S. Ruiz
Alexandria Rios Taylor

TODAY'S INSPIRED YOUNG LATINA VOL IV

This book is a compilation of stories from numerous people who have each contributed a chapter and is designed to provide inspiration to our readers.

It is sold with the understanding that the publisher and the individual authors are not engaged in the rendering of psychological, legal, accounting or other professional advice. The content and views in each chapter are the sole expression and opinion of its author and not necessarily the views of Fig Factor Media, LLC.

For more information, contact:

Fig Factor Media, LLC | www.figfactormedia.com
JJR Marketing, Inc. | www.jjrmarketing.com

Cover Design & Layout by Juan Manuel Serna Rosales
Printed in the United States of America

ISBN: 978-1-957058-94-8

We dedicate this book to young Latinas all over the world. Your stories matter and never be afraid to be your authentic self everywhere you go.

Table of Contents:

Acknowledgments 6

Preface by Neli Vazquez Rowland 7

Introduction by Jacqueline S. Ruiz & Alexandria Rios Taylor 11

YOUNG LATINA STORIES

BLANCA ACEVEDO 17

No Te Dejes Mija

DAINELIS RODRIGUEZ 23

Masita Goals: Learning to Achieve the Impossible

IZAR OLIVARES MENA 29

In Between the Lines

JESSICA GOMEZ 35

La Pequeña Dentista Que Si Pudo

FLOR CARABEZ 43

Tan Terca

ZENAIDA DE LA CRUZ 49

Let Your Faith Be Bigger Than Your Fear

ZULMA GUZMAN 55

Cultivating a Fearless Road Ahead

EMILY BASTIDA 63

Depender De Dios

DAYANA VILLAGRAN 69

Luck = (Hard Work) (Opportunities)

ELIANNE "ELY" BAHENA 75

Deja Que El Corazón y Tu Comunidad Sean Tu Guía

JAZMIN VALDERRAMA 83

Embrace Who You Are

ELIZABETH MARQUEZ 89

Life Changes

CYNTHIA PADILLA 95

Balancing It All

ALEXANDRA TURCIOS 101

Time is On No One's Side

MARIELA ESQUIVEL-RODRIGUEZ 109

Fuerza Sobre Debilidad

LORENA GUDINO 115

Manos al Fuego

NATALIA RAMIREZ 121

The Journey of Overcoming a Nightmare

ASHLI ENCARNACION 127

Keep Trying Until You Make It

CAROLINA SUERO 133

A Bundle of Sentiments

ITTATY AGUILAR-GUZMAN 139

Guerrera Reina

DEJHANAYRA ARGUETA 145

Becoming Me

About the Authors 152

Acknowledgments

This community has grown into what it is today not because of a single person, rather because of the love, support, and dedication of many people.

Thank you to the Fig Factor Media team for creating yet another beautiful impactful book: Gaby Hernández Franch, Shannon Mages, Juan Manuel Serna Rosales, and Izar Olivares.

Thank you to our Volume 1, 2, and 3 contributing authors. Your dedication to our mission is why we can continue to grow and expand our vision to serve more young Latinas.

Thank you to our friends and families for your unconditional support and love.

Thank you to the educators and mentors that work tirelessly to the younger generations and support and care so deeply for the youth. You are important and your work is invaluable.

Preface

NELI VAZQUEZ ROWLAND

Visionary, Philanthropist, Real Estate Developer, Serial Social Entrepreneur, Author

As I was reading the stories of these inspiring young Latinas, I was transported to my youth growing up as a young Latina. We have so much in common. I heard their voices, I felt their pain, challenges, hopes and dreams and celebrated their accomplishments along the way. They are all great story tellers and wise beyond their years.

I am the proud daughter of Carlos and Lucila Vazquez, they emigrated from Mexico in the 60's and like most immigrant stories, their story is one of sacrifice and overcoming many challenges to provide for their family of seven children on a single income. Growing up, our home always welcomed many other immigrant families, until they too were able to find their way. Their stories of courage, hard work, and compassion for helping others has always been an inspiration to me. Yet, growing up in Little Village, Chicago, I was exposed to many of the elements that many low income communities openly face such as gangs, drugs, and high drop out and teen pregnancy rates. I believe it was only through 'divine intervention' that I had a teacher, a friend's parent, and many others throughout my life that pulled me aside and took the time to guide and encourage me to stay on the right track especially when they saw me veering off in the wrong direction or with the wrong crowd. I'm grateful for others that went to bat and open doors for me in places that I never even knew existed. There was a time in my life when I almost dropped out of high school and because of so many standing in the gap, I became the first in my family to graduate from college and land a job as a stockbroker right out of college. At the time, it was a career that traditionally did not hire women and especially women of color. In fact, I was the only one I knew.

My life's journey—which includes my experiences, my education, and my environment growing up—has allowed me to overcome and embrace many of my own life's challenges and channel them to inform and fuel my efforts. This led me to become the pioneering architect of A Safe Haven, LLC and A Safe Haven Foundation. A Safe Haven Foundation has been recognized as one of the most compassionate, comprehensive, and integrated programs in the world intentionally designed to help people address and solve the root causes of poverty, addiction, and homelessness to help them achieve their highest God given potential. Our model and our work combine and applies my passion for business, real estate development, behavioral healthcare, social business enterprise, and making a lasting social impact. As a serial social entrepreneur and real estate developer, I am proud to have started and led the effort of building for profit businesses and nonprofits producing multi millions of dollars in revenues, creating jobs and providing thousands of people with work, and have it all be worth well over $100,000,000 today. More importantly, we have helped over 140,000 people, veterans and families with children and youth get their lives back on track. Blessed with financial success and in an effort to give back to be a good role model to my two young sons, Devin and Dylan, my husband Brian and I embarked on a quest to find the best charity to give a donation in a way that aligned with our values that was summed up in the old adage "give a man a fish and he eats for a day, teach a man to fish and he eats for a lifetime." I conducted extensive research and uncovered the fact that as a society our public and philanthropic systems were broken, disjointed, and financially unsustainable. I realized that while seemingly well intended, ultimately we were not truly focused on providing people in crisis a path to self-sufficiency and independence, but in too many cases causing them to fail and worse to become chronically and generationally dependent. When I started out, my husband and I put everything on the line. It took a huge vision, significant financial wherewithal, an unwavering commitment, and the powerful purpose of knowing that people's lives and their children's lives hung on the balance of our ability to successfully help them get on a path to independence and self-sufficiency.

After a few years of taking the personal risk and investing in building a better and more accountable solution, the demand we faced and our eventual ability to secure public financing allowed me to justify leaving my successful 13 year career in high finance to pursue a vision to create a one of a kind model designed to foster success. We did this by building several businesses that today are fully integrated and serve as components to our work. We have also been able to attract a high performing team of professionals who shared our passion and mission to help us accomplish our overall goal that today has helped over 140,000 people get access to individualized services such as behavioral healthcare, nutrition, education, job training, careers, and permanent housing. It is rewarding to know that the vast majority of them today live healthy and positive productive lives supporting themselves and their children.

There are lots of popular causes and movements that have come and gone throughout my life and much to my dismay the cause that I chose to pursue of helping the addicted, formerly incarcerated, and the homeless was perhaps the most highly stigmatized causes possible. Which meant that for almost two decades of our journey we got very little support, advocacy, or financial help from the public and government funding was also scarce. We went through many dark times which left us feeling alone, abandoned and financially strapped for many years working on behalf of the homeless and our cause, as a result. It is bittersweet because while we have helped transform the lives of thousands of people—and we tried to prevent it to getting to this point—but as we all can plainly see homelessness is visibly happening to people living on the streets everywhere in America today. So much of that perception is changing as people are starting to become better informed, and more understanding and compassionate about many of the reasons that led people to becoming homeless, such as preventable and manageable issues that can be healed with the right kind of help like mental health, addiction and poverty.

Throughout my career my motto has always been to "do well by doing good." I like to think that my curiosity and my uncanny ability to identify gaps in systems and trends early on, having a passion for business, and for helping and empowering people in crisis to become self-sufficient in a sustainable manner, I was able to live up to that goal.

Today is an exciting and pivotal moment in America. Just as I was inspired by generations before me, I am inspired by our youth today. They are living in a time when things are evolving and while they may be unfairly burdened with many of the mistakes that have been made by generations before them, the good news is that this is a reckoning moment and by working together and identifying, developing, and harnessing their gifts we have a golden opportunity to make things right for them and future generations. Throughout my career I had no real role models who could relate to my life experiences and background, so I read lots of books of successful people and surrounded myself with people that had accomplished a lot to learn from them and to be inspired. That said, I have also learned a lot from my critics. Whenever possible, I would encourage our youth to be protective of their time and spend it mostly with people who they mutually respect as positive influences, people they admire, love, believe, and bring out the best in them. Especially, when it comes to picking a spouse!

My advice is that whatever you choose to do to create your own legacy, pick a cause or career that you love and you cannot imagine not doing. Always be willing to grow, admit, and learn from your mistakes, and understand that succeeding at what you do, even if no one else knows about it, is your greatest reward. What I have learned as a pioneer and visionary is that not everyone sees what you see, nor will they always applaud or agree with what you are doing. Just remember, if it were easy, everyone would be doing it already and keep in mind if you're lucky, someone might notice what you did someday!

I remember being very surprised and almost shocked when I got the letter in the mail that I was being recognized in NYC by a leading women's advocacy organization for the work we were doing at A Safe Haven. Even today I am in awe, and super grateful to have been the subject of media stories, recognized and invited to speak by hundreds of different academic, business, and organizations of all types for our work all over the world, including Harvard and the White House, since then. I know that every time someone validates our efforts, it means that we are finally bringing the issue of homelessness out of the shadows and closer to the forefront of mainstream media. The hope is to becoming a priority humanitarian emergency issue for all of us to care about preventing and solving it, because we already know it can be done!

As mental health issues are having a serious impact on our youth today of all backgrounds, especially during the post pandemic era, I believe this book gives tremendous insights on how the authors were able to overcome negative experiences in their lives and use them as fuel to help them achieve wonderful goals because of them. It should be required reading in high schools or for anyone who is looking to be inspired across the country. Enjoy and be ready to be inspired! Cheers to the next generation of leaders!

Introduction

Four volumes of anything—much alone in a book series—is pretty amazing and special. It means growth and a continued demand to share stories. The fact is that right now we are creating the largest collection of the stories from young Latinas with this book series. That is something to celebrate and be proud of.

The number four is often connected and symbolizes stability, support, and a strong foundation. I think that is spot on with this fourth volume. All the stories shared in this book have a theme of strength within each authors' chapter and parallels the support and stability that our book series has created—a network of wonderful, inspiring, and leading young Latinas. We look forward to adding 21 more incredible young Latinas to our community.

I'm really honored to have the opportunity to walk this pathway with Alexandria Rios Taylor. Three years ago, we had no idea what this initial collaboration would turn into and create. It has opened doors to the next generation of Latinas and I'm thankful we get to do this together. I'm excited for the opportunities this book will bring for our young Latinas. The more energy we put into it the more we get out of it. It is a beautiful, amazing thing to witness the magix of this project.

What is most inspiring perhaps is being able to connect with these young ladies that have so much to offer to their families, their communities, and the world. To see some of those young ladies that were part of Volumes 1, 2, and 3, and see what they are doing now is incredible. Seeing what magix they are creating and how they are using their talents and qualities is beyond admirable. For Alexandria and I to be their madrinas, is truly an honor.

As the world continues to evolve, this topic is becoming much more relevant. Storytelling and connection among Latinas is so necessary and important. I am proud of the courage our young Latinas have to share and be vulnerable with their narratives. They understand how sharing their stories can create pathways for others to also share and connect with each other. Capturing these stories in this book is meant to guide and inspire the readers. It is a beautiful and honorable mission of sharing stories that need to be shared to ultimately create a positive impact in this world.

To our young contributing Latinas authors, thank you! You are our future leaders and we are honored to be your mentors. Thank you for saying yes to sharing your stories.

To our readers, thank you! For supporting us and reading these beautifully crafted stories—we appreciate you and hope you become inspired with these words and consider sharing your own story with the world.

Cheers to empowering young Latinas everywhere!

Love,
Alex and Jackie

YOUNG LATINA STORIES

NO TE DEJES MIJA

BLANCA ACEVEDO

"Invest in yourself and believe in yourself; we may be young, but we are also bilingual, educated, empowered, resilient, and creative."

I must have been eight or nine years old at the time, my mom and I were shopping at Walmart on a weekend night. That day we were looking for clear plastic bins. As usual my duty was to navigate our cart through the aisles as my mom shopped. I suddenly heard a big and tall woman yell angrily at me, "This is MY CART and these are MY BINS. You STOLE MY CART!"

I stood in silence watching her point her fingers at me while trying to take the cart away from me. I gripped on to the cart as hard as I could while frantically looking for my mom. "Mamiiiiii," I called out. I knew inside me that the lady was wrong and this was in fact my cart, but I could not gather the strength to even open my mouth and say any words to her.

"Que pasa?!" My mom peeked out from the aisle as she sees this woman yelling at me. "HEY NO LE ESTE GRITANDO. She is MY daughter; es MI CARRO esta loca. Shut up, shut up!" she yelled back. "You shut up lady. ES MI HIJA, shut up!" she repeated her words in broken English.

"Learn how to speak English!" the woman yelled back, as she slowly let the cart go and went on her way. This had to have been over 18 years ago, yet I still remember standing there feeling my heart beat increase every second while my cheeks and ears turned red. I realized that suddenly I had forgotten every English word I knew in my vocabulary. My mom then grabbed our cart and my hand and turned the other way, "Que vieja loca, tu no te dejas mija, nunca te dejes," she said to me.

I was born and raised in Mexico City, Mexico, until I was five years old when I was brought to Chicago, IL, to reunite with my mom and dad, both who had already immigrated here. I went to elementary and high school in my hometown of Cicero, IL. I was in ESL until 3rd grade and transitioned to full time English classes in 4th grade—this might explain why I suddenly forgot that I spoke English during the Walmart incident. As an ESL student, I faced the challenges of learning a new language while experiencing culture shock in a new country surrounded by new faces and a new world. Throughout the years it always felt like life kept throwing Walmart incidents at me. I would freeze, turn tomato red, forget my words, and yell out for my mom, "Mammiiiiii." Even now, at 26 years old, I still look out for my mom. It's always just been her and I.

Right before I entered college, my father had to travel back to Mexico permanently, to care for my grandma who was ill. This left my mom and I to deal with all college costs. I remember seeing my mom's face full of worry, concern, and guilt. "No te dejes mija," I reminded myself throughout the many hurdles I had to overcome during my academic education as an undocumented and first generation student.

I completed a master's degree in higher education leadership and graduated with a 4.0 GPA, while maintaining my full-time job and volunteer activities. This led me on to my professional career at the age of 21. For the last six years I have been able to wear the hat of associate director, teacher, coordinator, mentor, administrator, grant writer/editor, curriculum developer, national presenter, chair of hiring committees, chair of university roundtables, chair of Illinois TRIO legislation and education, chair of Women in STEM conferences, and most recently co-chair of the largest Latino festival in the Midwest.

"You look so young, how old are you?" I would get asked when attending professional conferences.

"Oh, YOU are the presenter?"

"Who do you work for?"

It constantly felt as if I was not being recognized in these spaces because of my age and instead was being seen as a shadow of others. Microaggressions came left and right regarding my age, my legal status, being Latina, first-gen, and low income.

A couple of months ago I got asked, "What do you want to be when you grow up?"

This almost made me chuckle because I thought to myself, "Am I not a grown up?" Not only was I asked this in front of a colleague, but also in front of the students I work with. Walmart moment—

there it was again, I froze, I looked at my colleague, she looked at me, I glanced over at my students.

"I am grown up and I am already pursuing the career I have worked for," I said. "As a matter of fact I am so involved in the community and in leadership roles that I'd like to invite you to meet to go over strategies that can help improve our enrollment and engagement." I was red; I was angry. Did he not mean it that way? I asked myself as I walked away. Despite my accomplishments and all I have done, I felt as if I was nine years old again.

Being a young Latina can bring many stereotypes that are not often talked about, but it also means that I am a young, courageous, and empowered Latina, that is no longer afraid to speak up or admit that I am mispronouncing words. I have learned to take deep breaths, speak up, and make sure I am seen and recognized for the work and value I bring to spaces. I share experiences with students and families that others may not—I understand the backgrounds, stories, and social impacts that are faced on a daily basis. I am bilingual, I am an educated Latina, I am also a proud immigrant, undocu/DACA professional, and, yes, I am a young professional.

Being young has allowed me to thrive in spaces bringing in creativity and innovation. I've learned to lead by example while pursuing my dreams and inspiring those around me. "No te dejes Mija." Now I tell my students and younger cousins invest in yourself and believe in yourself; we may be young, but we are also bilingual, educated, empowered, resilient, and creative. All around the world young Latinas like me can and will conquer these stereotypes, barriers, and adversities, and will continue to strive in workplaces, professional settings, academia, and everyday life.

THIS IS ME

My name is Blanca Acevedo. I am 26 years old and was born in Mexico City, Mexico. I am the Associate Director of the TRIO Upward Bound program at Northeastern Illinois University. I have a Master of Arts degree in Higher Education from the ENLACE Leadership Institute at NEIU. In my current role I develop 21st Century skills through the use of STEAM curriculum during afterschool enrichment in Chicago Public Schools. Additionally, I co-chair the largest Latino festival of the Midwest, Fiesta del Sol, in the Pilsen community, and co-chair the University Roundtable of Gamaliel of Metro Chicago.

My dreams for the future involve completing a doctoral program and continuing my career in higher education. I want to continue serving in roles that give back to my community.

MY TEN-YEAR PLAN:

1. To become 'Dra. Acevedo.'
2. To travel back to my home country and many other places of the world without limitations.
3. To work as the VP or President of a college—while also encouraging cultural arts projects in higher education, such as traditional Mexican folklore dance curriculum.

MASITA GOALS: LEARNING TO ACHIEVE THE IMPOSSIBLE

DAINELIS RODRIGUEZ

"Anything you want in life, tienes que luchartelo (you need to work for it). No matter what it is, tú puedes logarlo (you can achieve it)."
- Mami and Papi

I was born in Isla de la Juventud, Cuba, during "El Periodo Especial" (The Special Period). This period occurred during the early 90's. The island of Cuba and its people were suffering through an unfortunate societal and economic crisis. Many of the basic necessities such as food and energy were being rationed to the population. My parents would describe the stories of the daily apagones (blackouts) and how the food would sometimes not be enough. Both my parents were university graduates. Mami was a social worker and Papi was an agronomist. Despite having good jobs, their monthly salary was not sufficient. To generate more income, my parents would sell vegetables door-to-door to buy more basic goods and a few treats here and there.

Although I was born during El Periodo Especial, I was

born with my papi's appetite and love for all kinds of food. My nickname in Cuba was Masita (little dough). For me, it was (and still is) a joy to eat and savor every piece of food on my plate. From soups to my favorite arroz con frijoles (rice and beans), I ate it all. My love of food did not change even when I moved to the United States at the tender age of four. What did change was my physique. My weight was increasing… a lot. When I started school for the first time, I was the tallest and the biggest (weight-wise) amongst all of my classmates in kindergarten.

Transitioning to middle school was no breeze. Not only had I gained more weight (I was weighing around 150 pounds at just 10 years old), but my weight was one of the targets of a lot, and I repeat, A LOT of bullying. I remember this one distinct boy who would always call me names and throw things at me. My weight along with the constant bullying deteriorated my confidence and self-esteem.

Fast forward to high school, my weight kept increasing. I was now weighing 166 pounds at just 14 years old. At this moment, I was not happy with how I looked and to make matters worse, my Quinceañera (Sweet 15) was only a few months away and I didn't feel the least bit pretty to wear a gown. To top it all off, my primary care physician declared that I was overweight. I felt disgusted with myself.

As my quince (15th birthday) approached, my parents and I drove all the way to Miami, Florida to meet with a photographer at his studio. When we got there, my parents and I chose the backgrounds for the photo sessions and I had to try on some dresses for the photoshoot. None of the dresses in his studio fit me. NADA! I was mortified. To add onto my mortification, the photographer takes it upon himself to say (very loudly, because Cubans do not have inside voices) that I had to lose weight in front of a lot of people. I was so embarrassed! My eyes watered, but I dared not shed a tear.

On the car ride home, I thought back to a conversation I had with my mom when I was in middle school. It was a day that my mom caught me crying in my room and asked me what was wrong.

I said, "Estoy gorda (I'm fat)."

She said to me, *"Si tú crees que tú estás gorda, tienes dos opciones: o sigues llorando y sintiendote así o cambias y te enfrentas el problema (if you feel that you are fat, you have two options: either you can keep crying and stay as you feel, or you can change how you feel by tackling the issue)."*

The next day I took action. I began to exercise every day, starting first with 30 minutes and then slowly increased it to one hour. Every evening I walked the treadmill and did abdomen workouts. I also went on a diet, but not as you would think. I love my Cuban food and kept eating my arroz con frijoles, just in smaller portions. I began to eat my dulces (treats) in moderation such as my delicious pastelitos (pastries) and I removed sodas and fast food from my diet, unless I wanted to, but that was on rare occasions—maybe once a month if that.

I did this for two years. For my quinces, I was able to lose 11 pounds. This was my first achievement as I was now weighing 155 pounds. However, when I turned 17, I went down to 130 pounds. I HAD LOST 25 POUNDS! This was a huge accomplishment. I, for the first time in my life, was able to look in the mirror and speak positive words to myself. I exuded so much confidence throughout the process that I rebuilt my self-esteem. I felt delighted in my own skin and I was GLOWING. I was able to accomplish a goal I had set my mind to and it felt amazing.

When I encounter a difficult time in my life for a goal I want to achieve, I look back at how I was able to lose 36 pounds in two years. Losing weight for me seemed impossible, but knowing that I was able to do it made me see that nothing is impossible. Of course, throughout my weight loss journey, there were times that I didn't exercise and had more dulces than I was supposed to, but I looked back at my goal and felt more determined to get back up and keep going.

As my Mami and Papi always said, "*Anything you want in life, tienes que luchartelo (you need to work for it). No matter what it is, tú puedes logarlo (you can achieve it).*"

THIS IS ME

I was born in Isla de la Juventud, Cuba, and came to the United States when I was four years old. I grew up in Florida alongside my mom, dad and younger sister. Growing up in a Cuban household while in the United States was challenging but came with a lot of laughter and love. Having a passion for storytelling, content creation and helping others, I utilize my knowledge, resources, and Cuban culture to help others who face struggles with language barriers and legal battles. Siempre positiva y con una sonrisa brillante!

MY TEN-YEAR PLAN:

1. Publish my bilingual stories in a book.
2. Create and operate a business where I can help incoming immigrants and those already in the country with immigration assistance.
3. Expand and flourish the design business I have with my sister internationally.

IN BETWEEN THE LINES

IZAR OLIVARES MENA

"She chose to judge me not for the reading skills I lacked, but because my mother tongue was different than the rest of the class."

I never thought that I would be working in the publishing industry. I thought that I would have a career in medicine, like I had initially planned—but that's a story for another day. What I never realized was that my love for reading was something I would eventually make a career out of. I knew I had a gift for understanding the written word, but it was always only ever a hobby.

I was born in Monterrey, Nuevo León, Mexico, in July 1997. When I was two and a half years old, my family moved to Cicero, IL, sharing a three-story house with two of my dad's sisters and their families, who moved there before us. From the moment that I began to speak, my first language was Spanish. Growing up in a Mexican household, it was our primary language. Though it wasn't a problem in preschool, it became one in grade school since English was now the main language. The majority of first grade I was placed in bilingual classes as I slowly adjusted to learning and speaking only English at school. It took a couple of years to get used to it, but now I like to think that I've finally mastered the language, but in return lost some Spanish vocabulary as I grew older.

I have always loved to read. I blame my long-term obsession on two individuals, who gave me completely opposite experiences. The first person was my 4th grade teacher. I don't particularly like to use the word "hate" to describe what I feel for her, but I like to think it's pretty close. I don't hold a hatred for her for what she told me, but instead how she said it. She told me I was too stupid to read. *Stupid.* That's the word she chose to use to tell a nine-year-old bilingual girl that was still getting used to reading in English that she wasn't meeting the 4th grade reading standards. Some may say, "Maybe she didn't mean it that way," but she knew my background and she chose to judge me not for the reading skills I lacked, but because my mother tongue was different than the rest of the class.

I admit that I struggled to read a little, but that wasn't an excuse for her to approach the situation in the way that she did. This was one of the many moments that she made me feel like I was lower than the rest of my classmates. That year I was constantly picked on by her, getting yelled at for taming my messy hair with water in the bathroom or for unintentionally getting answers wrong. This was the lowest I had felt—to the point where it made me cry. It even made my mom leave the car running in the middle of the pick-up line to go and yell at her.

Almost two decades later, I can't forget what I felt that day because it was one of the first moments where I felt like I didn't belong. I still think of this day, not out of anger, but as a reminder that if I was able to overcome something like this at such a young age, whatever obstacle that I would face in the future would be just as easy to rise above. Now, I think about how hard it was for my parents to adapt when they moved to the US, leaving their family behind and speaking only a handful of English, but raising my brothers and I the best that they could. In a way, this experience is a constant reminder that my culture is different than others and that being raised in the US has brought many struggles, but that doesn't mean I would trade it for the world.

The other person I owe my infatuation with books to is Enjolique, my tutor. She was the person that I, still to this day, am grateful to have met. Every time we would meet, it was at a library which, in the end, became one of favorite places to be—besides Barnes and Noble. Though her mission was to have me read at grade level, she did much more than that. She introduced me to books and words in a way that I had never experienced. From her I learned that books can hold a deeper meaning than they initially have and by reading in between the lines, you could find them. Despite knowing my low reading level, Enjolique challenged it because she saw the potential that I had within.

With every book we would read there was a lesson to be learned and she would make sure I knew what it was. I still remember one of the first books she had me read: *The Tale of Despereaux* by Kate DiCamillo. The book she gave me was 32 chapters long. As a 4th grader, I thought she was nuts, yet I finished it and I loved every moment.

One of the lessons that she taught me was to never watch a movie before reading the book because the book will always hold more details than the movie ever will, no matter how small the details were. She had me test this out with *James and the Giant Peach* by Roald Dahl and as soon as I finished the book, she gifted me the movie and she was absolutely right; movies are NEVER as good as the book.

From that point on, books became my safe haven; something I could always go back to no matter what and gave me the adventure that I often searched for. I always had my nose buried in a book to where I inherited the name "little bookworm" by one of my mom's coworkers. Everywhere we went, a book came with me, reading it at every chance I could get. I would finish a book in a day or two and without a breath in between move on to the next one.

The love I grew for books was something that I have never forgotten and to which I am now proud to say that I have made into a career, despite what my 4th grade teacher had said. As low as she made me feel that day, I didn't let her get the best of me and for that I would like to thank her. Without her I would have never met Enjolique, nor ended up pursuing a career doing what I love most and sharing with others how to cherish books just as much as I do.

THIS IS ME

I currently work as an author concierge for Fig Factor Media where I have the pleasure of guiding authors through the process of bringing their books to life. I recently became an author of the WordPOWER series Spanish Edition book, *Soñar,* in July 2022. As an aspiring writer and avid reader, I hope to touch others' hearts and show them the true beauty of books and words. More specifically, I hope to publish a series of children's books to ignite a love for reading in them as well and show them the value of books at a young age.

MY TEN-YEAR PLAN:

1. Write a series of children's books.
2. Travel overseas (specifically Greece and Italy).
3. Master my editorial skills by taking classes.

JESSICA GOMEZ

"Sí tú puedes. Yes, you can."

Six of us lived in the Gomez household. We lived in chaos, but that prepared me for obstacles in the real world. My dad, a hardworking carpenter, gave birth to four kids with my mom, an even harder-working homemaker. Jessie, then Jackie, then Jo, then Julius. We were all so different, but the best of friends. I loved my siblings. As the eldest daughter, I decided that it was my job to protect them from the dangers we faced.

I spent my childhood translating at appointments and editing my dad's work reports, as my astounding English grades appointed me the most proficient in the house. As the oldest, I dealt with my feelings alone. No one could know how sad and tired I always felt. It was my job to be strong and brave for the entire family.

Despite the distractions at home and the many distractions in my brain, I remained a bright student. I loved school. I often found myself longing for a life filled with knowledge and happiness like the women I learned about. I bet Amelia Earhart didn't make herself throw up after eating a bowl of ice cream. Did Marie Curie deal with the occasional emotional abuse from her family, too? Eh, probably not. But they were both examples of the type of woman I so badly wanted to be.

After school, I liked to hide in my room while dreaming of college, even if I didn't know how to get there. Growing up in a White neighborhood allowed statistics and stereotypes to weigh me down. Despite the odds being against me, something clicked—I was destined to create with my hands. Finding a career that peaked my many interests seemed impossible, but once my braces were removed, I knew I wanted to pursue dentistry.

College! Nothing prepared me for the next four years.

I grew up in a White neighborhood with White friends and White teachers and White doctors and White boyfriends. Marquette University, the school I chose, was pretty damn White. This was nothing new, but what shocked me was the overt racism that spewed from my new friends' lips.

Overhearing racist conversations made me feel more alienated than ever. My friends claimed to care about me, yet they thought Trump's Wall was the next best thing for our country since Edison invented the lightbulb.

No matter how rough and confusing college became, I never lost sight of my dream. Long nights of partying followed by early morning trips to the library became my new normal. Hours of writing papers and memorizing chemical reactions exhausted me. When I look back at this part of my life, I often wonder how

I ever made it out alive. As if studying wasn't draining enough, I managed to work full-time through undergrad.

In January 2020 BCE (Before COVID Era), I traveled to Panama for a Marquette Dental Brigades trip. The organization provides free dental care while we students assist local dentists. Although I spent months excitedly fundraising for the trip, I anxiously sobbed to my mom the night before, "I don't want to go. I don't know anyone. I won't even like it!"

That week just so happened to be the best week of my life. I practiced Spanish, fell in love with public health, and met my best friends. When we returned to Milwaukee it was obvious that our bonds weren't breaking anytime soon. My weird tooth obsession and my inappropriate sense of humor were… accepted by my friend group. Encouraged, even! My Brigade friends helped me find light in my personal, constant cloudiness. Milwaukee slowly turned into the home I spent years dreaming of—a home where I felt like I belonged.

As COVID shut down society, my motivation and grades plummeted. Fast. The COVID restrictions at school were strict. Constant isolation, undiagnosed ADHD, and the smallest ounce of the will to live were all key ingredients in this recipe for disaster. And that recipe was brewing all right.

Procrastination became my only study tactic. Assignments and exams were all left to the last second with zero effort put in. I never turned down a reason to party or to smoke until I felt like I was on another planet. My three-year long-distance relationship fell apart, so I convinced myself that excessive physical attention from other people was what I needed to fill my void. I was miserable. Misery was me.

Much to *nobody's* surprise, I ended the semester with a D+ in Organic Chemistry.

My only solution was to retake the class. I signed up for a summer session and finished with a B! Operation Dr. Jessie was back on track again... until I learned that I couldn't afford the class. I faced withdrawal from Marquette University until I paid it off.

I couldn't believe it. What was I supposed to do? Where would I get this money from? I silently prayed for the first time in years as I dialed my dad's number.

Padre Nuestro, que estás en el cielo...

I prepared myself to deliver the bad news, "I can't register for my last semester or graduate because of this remaining balance. And, no, financial aid doesn't cover it. I already tried."

I messed up big time. My dad was definitely going to make that known.

"The class was around six thousand dollars," I whispered through tears. I felt horrible. Guilty. I knew my parents didn't have this type of money just laying around, but this class was required for dental school applications. Since FAFSA can't be applied to summer terms, my dad and I applied for private loans. We were denied time after time.

How do I explain this mess to my friends? My life rapidly fell apart, and it was all my fault. Time was running out. I was back in Panama for the second time ridden with anxiety. All I could think about was finding a way to start school next week.

In a desperate attempt to re-enroll me, my dad withdrew the amount owed from his retirement savings. It worked.

On May 22, 2022, I graduated from Marquette University with an Honors Bachelors' degree. I majored in Psychology with a minor in Biological Sciences. Within four years, my momentum never stopped. I traveled to a national research conference to present my work from the lab. I won countless awards for leadership on campus. I even attended a competitive dental education enrichment program through the Association of American Medical Colleges, and I soon found myself as the lead dental assistant at my clinic! Giving up or slowing down are never options for me, not until I become a Doctor of Dental Surgery. The first in my family, but hopefully not the last.

I inherit my motivation and strong sense of community from my Latinx ancestors. The Indigenous Mexicans developed exceptional manual dexterity skills by making intricate pieces of jewelry so that I might be quick and nimble with my fingers in the clinic. My father, like many Latino dads, spent his life drilling into and putting up drywall to prepare me for filling a cavity while restoring the composite wall.

Today, only 6% of practicing dentists in the United States are Hispanic. Latinx and Hispanic communities deserve accessible oral care and representation. I believe that every human deserves the right to affordable and adequate dental care. I am ready to make that happen. I strive to make a change for the Latinx community inside and outside of dentistry.

My biggest piece of advice? Be your own biggest fan, because if you aren't then who else will be? Think about what you want for yourself, what you need to make you happy, and just do it. It's easy to lose ourselves in this fast-paced society, but I promise you that nothing is more freeing than confidence and self-love.

THIS IS ME

I graduated from Marquette University as an Honors program student majoring in Psychology and minoring in Biological Sciences. I'm currently in the process of applying to dental schools! If I'm not dental assisting, you can find me exploring Milwaukee with my friends, hanging out with my cat, or going to Bucks' games.

I would also like to thank three amazing women who have gotten me where I am today: my mother, Sofia D'Acquisto, and Dr. Claire Kirchhoff.

MY TEN-YEAR PLAN:

1. I plan to write a novel sometime in the future.
2. Start a scholarship fund for Latina women going into the dental field.
3. I would love to have my own personal library in my future home!

FLOR CARABEZ

"Being terca can be a good thing."

I was sitting on the edge of my bed on a hot summer day in Chicago. I had been sitting there for what felt like an hour, procrastinating opening the letter I had received from Northern Illinois University. A year ago, around this time, I was excited counting down the days until my move-in day into the dorms. Today I was dreading opening the letter where they would formally kick me out.

I had hit rock bottom and I was stressing over how my parents would react.

After opening the letter, the only feeling I had left was worry.

You see, the last twelve months of my life had been filled with stress and heartache. As if navigating college alone wasn't stressful enough, I also dealt with a traumatic breakup and found myself mediating my parents' marriage.

Why do parents expect the oldest sibling to solve their marital problems?

I had been walking around depressed, undiagnosed.

Instead of gaining the freshman 15, I lost 30 pounds. Instead of going to class, I would sleep because I was too busy crying and feeling worthless and alone at night. My mental state was so bad that my roommate didn't feel comfortable leaving me alone.

When I finally gathered the courage to tell my parents, my dad immediately expressed his disappointment. "You fucked up. All that partying you were doing instead of doing what you were supposed to do is why you got kicked out. What are you gonna do now? What am I supposed to tell my friends?!"

Dude, what am I supposed to do with my life?

I didn't have the courage to tell him the truth and still don't. I responded, "I don't know; I'll figure it out. I'll probably just go to Daley for now."

"Well, you better figure something out because you're not about to stay here, not doing anything with your life. You fucked up," he repeated.

Since Facebook had just started, I was using the platform as a diary. My followers were aware of my breakup and my experience at NIU. When my dad brought up my *partying*, he was referring to the pictures I had uploaded with my friends on Facebook. He didn't know that my friends had to pick out my clothes, do my hair and makeup, and force me to go out with them so I wouldn't cry alone in my dorm.

After I confessed my dismissal to my parents, I posted a status about it on Facebook. Immediately, the director of the

Upward Bound program I was a part of in high school sent me a direct message expressing concern. For my breakup, she convinced me to turn my heartache into anger. Converting this emotion was difficult, but it helped me focus on my academic journey. At the time, she was an Assistant Dean at Triton College, so she was quickly able to help me navigate my transfer to Daley College.

Once I enrolled at Daley, I started looking for clubs to join. Luckily, the college was just beginning a soccer team and needed players. I immediately joined and started attending practice. Soccer ended up being my outlet and was the only reason I was allowed to leave my house (other than for school or errands for my parents). I was the first to show up to practice and the last to leave. I was doing so well that the college even offered me a scholarship!

Or so I thought...

I was at an evening club soccer game that same summer when I received a voicemail from my coach stating that not only was my scholarship revoked, but I was going to be redshirted that season because of my academic dismal at NIU. Despite my fear of crying in public, I broke into a complete sob in front of my team during halftime.

They all huddled over me, consoling me while my dad asked one of them what was happening.

The car ride home was completely silent.

I got home, sat on the edge of the bed with swollen eyes, and felt anger radiate through my body.

I refuse to let this shit keep happening. I worked so hard to be on the team and earn this scholarship, and this NIU shit is still haunting me?!

That night I let anger feed my stubbornness.

I will get that scholarship back and play on that soccer team. I don't care how hard I have to try.

Despite being red-shirted, I continued participating in practice and attending the games. My affiliation with the team provided the supportive community I needed at the time. All athletes had an academic and financial aid advisor assigned to them. Because I was focused on regaining my scholarship and athletic eligibility, I took advantage of these privileges and became proactive with my academics. I started meeting with my academic advisor frequently to ensure I was on track. I courageously asked my professors for help during and after class. I found a tutor for math and science, because those were the courses I struggled with the most and I joined study groups.

After my first year at Daley, I became co-captain of the soccer team, regained my scholarship, and was added to the Dean's List. Out of curiosity, I also decided to apply to my initial dream school (University of Illinois Urbana-Champaign) and reapply to NIU. To my surprise, U of I admitted me, while NIU rejected me. *Pero soy tan terca,* I decided to decline my admission to U of I and complete my Associate's at Daley to return to NIU. I felt that I had a bone to pick with NIU and I wanted to prove to myself and the university that I was more than capable of graduating.

Hitting rock bottom forced me to trust my learning abilities, stop seeking validation from my parents, and self-advocate. Two and a half years later, I earned my Associate's in Arts and returned to NIU. Today I hold my Bachelor's degree from NIU, Master's degree from UIC, and am working on my Doctorate from National Louis University. Being *terca* can be a good thing.

THIS IS ME

Currently, I am employed full-time at National Louis University (NLU) as a Senior Success Coach and adjunct professor. I am also earning my Doctorate of Education in Higher Education Leadership at NLU. On the side, I run Esperanza Equity Consulting LLC and teach Zumba classes.

I want to continue sharing my stories in hopes that they will provide light for someone who feels they have hit rock bottom. I also want to continue advocating for students like me to receive the academic and emotional support they need to be successful.

MY TEN-YEAR PLAN:

1. Become a well-known Latina author.
2. Have Esperanza Equity Consulting thrive so I can work it full-time.
3. Live somewhere surrounded by nature.

LET YOUR FAITH BE BIGGER THAN YOUR FEAR

ZENAIDA DE LA CRUZ

"Do it scared."

As a Latina who is a first-generation college student attending a predominantly white institution, I have faced social barriers in my educational journey and learned how my upbringing has defined who I am. At home in Idaho, I live in a predominantly Hispanic/Latin community and in high school my classmates and educators reflected my identities. I attended a public school where I was heavily involved in extracurriculars and thrived academically. My parents always taught me and my brother that education opens many doors for you and can change your life. I believed my parents, but I never fully understood just how education and taking risks could—and eventually would—change my life.

When I was a sophomore in high school, I began to focus on what my plan was after graduation. I always knew I wanted to go to college, but never thought much about where and what I would study. I just figured I would get my associates at the local community college and figure the rest out later. One of the first steps I took in preparing myself for college was applying to and joining TRIO Upward Bound. TRIO Upward Bound is a college preparatory program for students who will be first generation college students and/or fall under a certain socioeconomic status. As I progressed through the Upward Bound program, I began to recognize that, although my hometown is special to me, I have the potential to achieve something bigger outside of it. I often thought, "What else is out there for me to explore?"

In my first two years in the Upward Bound program, I was blessed to visit many colleges, but none of them ever spoke to me. That was until the summer of 2019, going into my senior year, when I visited a university in Washington. I loved the small community, religious affiliation, and the liberal arts aspect of studies. From then onward, I looked for everything I loved in that university in other schools and submitted my applications.

It wasn't too long after that I had been accepted to all but one of the universities I applied to. I remember feeling overwhelmed with pride and gratitude. This was the hardest I had pushed myself outside of regular academics and all my hard work had paid off. At the same time, I was also very nervous. I didn't know what to expect. Two of the universities that I was accepted to, which also happened to be my top two preferred schools, awarded me with substantial financial aid that would make it very possible for me to attend either one along with my scholarships. The only issue was that one school was the university in Washington that I fell in love with the summer prior and the other was a university across the country that I had never visited in Pennsylvania.

In the process of choosing between schools, I had to figure out what I wanted in my undergraduate experience. Initially, I remember saying I would attend school in Washington because going across the country just wasn't an option. But it was. I was coming up with excuses not to say yes because I was afraid of the unknown. While I really wanted to challenge myself with this new experience, I didn't want to leave the close proximity of my family. I knew that going to Pennsylvania was an amazing opportunity that I could have never imagined for myself, but I was scared. I feared that I would hate it and be too far from home to come back. I feared I would love it and want to start a life there. I wouldn't see my family as often. I didn't know if I was ready for such a drastic change, and I only had so much time to make a decision.

Amidst this decision making, I was also going through a break up. I was with someone who was going through depression and I was the only person who took care of him. I recognized how drained I had become over the years and ended the relationship. It took a huge toll on me, but I knew I couldn't let anyone hold me back, especially when making decisions about college.

After much reflection and many long talks with my Upward Bound advisor, Josh Engler, and my family, I decided to commit to the university in Pennsylvania, Villanova University. I never felt like I had to prove anything to anyone, so making this decision was only about what I wanted—to show other students in my high school and younger family members that it could be done and know that if I could do it, so could they. I also knew that if I didn't choose Villanova, I wasn't going to reach my full potential and I owed that to myself.

In that moment I learned that even if a decision is hard to make and you are afraid, most of the time it's the right one. I spent almost four years in a relationship and after the breakup, this was the first time that I stopped letting others hold me back. Take the leap, even if you're scared or don't feel ready, do it anyway. The truth is you'll never feel 100% ready, but you can't stand in the way of your progress and growth.

The summer before college I was really excited to start my journey at Villanova, but I was also sad to be leaving my hometown. I spent the rest of my summer with my loved ones and prepared myself for college as best as I could.

In the fall of 2020, I flew to Philadelphia, Pennsylvania, with my parents for first-year move-in at Villanova. It was a beautiful feeling being able to experience this moment together. The two people who have always motivated me and supported me were there with me. Even though they have never been to college or experienced moving into a residence hall, they still found every way to support me and that meant the world to me. This was something that we went through together and my only wish was that my brother was there too. The week they spent in Philadelphia went by quickly and before I knew it, I was hugging them goodbye. I remember my heart breaking and feeling alone, but knowing that eventually I would be alright.

My first year at Villanova was tough. I was dealing with the transition from high school to college, but also from Idaho to Pennsylvania amidst a pandemic. I met my professors through Zoom classrooms and was missing the physical relationship I was used to. I transitioned from a predominantly Hispanic/Latin community to a predominantly white community. While I didn't think this would impact me, I struggled to find my place even within the Hispanic/Latin community. I would connect with other Hispanic/Latin students, but I never felt fully connected to them. I was also experiencing the differences between the culture in Idaho compared to Pennsylvania. Most importantly, I was navigating living on my own over 2,000 miles away from home and everything I knew. As a result of my huge transition, I would often be anxious and homesick; but I couldn't just go home, I had to face it. I put most of my energy into my schoolwork and would remind myself of my purpose. While my first year was difficult in many ways, I slowly found my way and created space for myself on campus.

Fast forward to the present, I am now a junior at Villanova University. Despite the culture shock through my first year and a lot of homesickness, I'd like to think that I've excelled academically and socially. Although I still get nervous being the only Latina in class or being the only person from Idaho at my university, I no longer let my fear hold me back. My journey to and through college has only proved that fear is inevitable, but you must let your faith be bigger. You must know that the "perfect" time to decide doesn't exist. Your time is now. Don't let fear stand in the way of your growth. Do it scared.

THIS IS ME

My name is Zenaida De La Cruz, and I am the proud daughter of Hector and Julie De La Cruz, who are my rocks through and through. I am a Latina who is a first-generation college student attending Villanova University studying Sociology and Criminology with a minor in Public Administration. I am passionate about studying human relationships and the way institutions impact society. I serve on the Latin American Student Organization (LASO) Executive Board, as a Resident Assistant on campus, and am a proud member of Lambda Theta Alpha Latin Sorority, Incorporated. I believe it is my vocation to cultivate and create spaces for people like me to be able to exist and succeed in places where we're not expected to be. Most of all, I aspire to be for others who I needed as a young girl because representation matters.

MY TEN-YEAR PLAN:

1. To become financially stable enough to retire my parents.

2. To positively impact diversity in higher education by starting a scholarship for rising first-generation college juniors/seniors.

3. To find my person and start a family of my own.

CULTIVATING A FEARLESS ROAD AHEAD

ZULMA GUZMAN

"The most beautiful views come after the most challenging climbs."
- Author Unknown

It all began in the city of Guadalajara in Mexico, where at the age of two I moved to La Salle, a small town located 94 miles southwest of Chicago with approximately 9,000 people. I was raised to be a small-town girl with dreams of being a businesswoman since the age of ten.

On a gloomy afternoon at Buffalo State Park in 2019, I looked at the river, where I found myself distracted from who I aspired to be with no self-confidence, sour friendships, and a toxic relationship. Time was not on my side because I was only a few months away from relocating to Chicago to pursue my degree in finance, and I needed to figure out who I was along with my tranquility.

The idea of leaving my hometown scared me and missing out on my siblings growing up. It was an era full of insecurity and a roller coaster of emotions. When the day arrived, I helped my parents load all of my belongings onto the burgundy Honda Pilot. Onto the road we went as I stared out the window, watching cornfields turn into tall buildings, trains going in different directions, and the streets filled with people in the beautiful city of Chicago.

To be where I am today, there were various bumps on the road. I felt at my lowest point right before moving to Chicago. After being involved in toxic relationship for several years, I found the courage to close the chapter. I knew I needed a lot of inner work after multiple counts of emotional abuse and letting myself get controlled, manipulated, and disrespected. I was lost and distracted, while trying to stay focused on my educational goals and figuring out what everyone calls being a first-generation student.

On the car ride to Chicago, my thoughts were racing. What if fail to make my parents proud? What if I don't make any friends? I left my hometown feeling nervous, excited, and full of fear, as all I had known was how to be a small-town girl. It was the beginning of my self-discovery journey while learning to navigate the city of Chicago.

Being a transfer student and coming from a small town made me feel like I had been living in a small hole, missing out on various opportunities the city had to offer. During my first few months in Chicago, I often compared myself to others. Many students were well advanced on their college journey with various internship offers and advanced finance classes, which made me feel like I was behind. I started joining every organization I could, applying everywhere, and doing extensive research every night. My college roommate Maritza, who became my best friend, would come with me to the 24-hour Starbucks around 10 p.m. and we would leave around 7 a.m. after spending the night studying and doing career research.

While I was learning new things, I needed to still figure out who I wanted to be and build my self-confidence. I would often doubt my abilities to the point that it held me back from several opportunities. In early 2020, I joined a sorority whose values were in alignment, specifically on self-confidence. I participated in the Fig Factor Core 16 in the fall of 2020, a program dedicated to unleashing the amazing future Latina leaders. Through Fig Factor, I met Ivys, who taught me the importance of taking care of myself when it came to my mental and physical health, while still being conscious of my goals—a key component to living a happy life.

Through different organizations, I started to build my community, a community of friends that were ambitious in many aspects of life. In a matter of months, I found myself leaning into every opportunity or event that I could attend. One day at a virtual networking event, one of the panelists named Yoly stood out to me as she had a 20-year career in banking and was a long-time philanthropist. I knew I had to connect with her as I aspired to be in banking and getting involved in the community. I scheduled a call with her via LinkedIn, and the rest was history as she became one of the biggest influences in my life. She introduced me to women in leadership in the banking industry, which turned into a ripple effect of other women empowering me to pursue my career in banking.

After conducting multiple interviews in the banking industry, I received a call with the opportunity to relocate to Atlanta, Georgia, to start my career in commercial banking. I recall receiving Melissa's instant phone call, an admirable woman in banking, where she shared her relocation experiences with the same bank inspiring me to accept and relocate. I accepted the offer before mentioning it to my family. I was thrilled to be with a banking institution that is growing in the southeast.

People would ask me if I had friends or family in Georgia, and my answer was no. The only thing I was sure of was that I was on my way to Atlanta to start my career in commercial banking. I read, "We're glad Georgia is on your mind," on the welcome sign to Georgia on a perfect fall day. It was the beginning of who my ten-year-old self had envisioned as a businesswoman.

My passion for starting my career in banking was bigger than the fear of living alone in another state, where I knew no one. If I had done it in Chicago, coming from a small town where I started from ground zero, I could do it all over again. Except this time, I was aware of who I was and who I wanted to be— focused and driven to make an impact in every room I walked in.

I recall calling my parents to give them the news that I was moving. My parents, mentors, and friends were beyond proud and supportive of this new journey to Atlanta, which I call home today.

As I navigate the city of Atlanta, I reflect on the curveballs thrown at me that gave me the wisdom to be exactly where I was meant to be. From La Salle to Chicago, and now Atlanta, I continue to gain a wider view of the world.

Awareness was the first step towards my self-growth journey as I let myself feel out emotions rather than trying to avoid them. The importance of who makes up my environment is crucial to living a fulfilled life as I leaned on those for support and to help me level up. Building community with others who are in alignment with me was vital to my success thus far, and as someone once said, "Your network determines your net-worth."

An important component was giving myself time to reflect, be grateful, and maintain a positive outlook, which led to having a powerful mindset giving me clarity and focus on my goals. The pain led to growth and wisdom, as I transformed into a better version of myself discovering a passion to serve the community while making an impact and delivering value. The setbacks I have experienced are a contributor to my daily motivation. It was an awakening to my life's purpose. I am evolving and ready to embrace the next chapter of my life.

THIS IS ME

I am a Financial Analyst at BMO Commercial Bank, where I help provide solutions to meet the financing needs of private and publicly traded companies in the Southeast along with portfolio management. I was raised in La Salle County in Illinois, where I obtained my associates degree at Illinois Valley Community College and a B.S. in Finance from DePaul University in Chicago. Throughout my college journey and post college life thus far, I have held various leaderships roles and initiatives in the community around women in leadership, professional development, and community outreach.

I aspire to continue to mentor and empower young women to unlock their full potential. Through a successful career in the financial services, I hope to maximize value for the continuous growth of my client's businesses. I will pave the way for many other generations to come while increasing financing opportunities for all in the commercial space.

MY TEN-YEAR PLAN:

1. Launch an impactful program to equip young women with resources to build wealth at an early stage to reach financial independence.

2. To obtain my CFA and tap into the venture capital space to help entrepreneurs take their business to the next level.

3. To obtain a successful career trajectory in banking with a focus on leadership, increased portfolio size, and value driven.

EMILY BASTIDA

"He restoreth my soul: he leadeth me in the paths of righteousness for his name's sake." -Psalm 23:3

For some Latino families, education is placed as a priority for the purposes of improving our family's socioeconomic status. My immediate family made no exception as education was one of our motivators. Education was such a big factor in my life that when I was a 3rd grade student I started crying because I could not complete my assignments due to the language barrier. Until recently as a university student, at 24 years old, I barely can pass some of my classes and I cry out of frustration.

These circumstances may be hard to change by ourselves as humans, but with God's help everything is possible—not just for me, but for many people throughout time that have placed their faith in God to aid them towards a solution. God has corrected me and I was able to see that I was in the wrong and it was painful to see my errors. I had an ego problem and I wanted to be treated in a special way and I acted out in a very aggressive manner. Before Christianity I was just a believer. I did not even attend church at all.

As the eldest daughter in my family, I have been given the privilege to create a path for my younger siblings to follow with my education. As I found hardship in my educational and professional journey I questioned, like Job, why all these situations had to occur specifically to me as if not everyone struggles with something. I found my life took a turning point when I started transferring to university in the fall of 2019.

I remember visiting the campus a few years back with my wonderful mama. It was a very emotional time for us because we were both excited, but worried about me going to college and how we were going to pay for it. Mi mama, what an amazing mujer, she has worked hard to provide for me and my hermanitos and although I have seen the tiredness in her eyes she brushes it off. Thanks to God's will I was able to secure a scholarship that would allow me to attend the private institution I currently attend.

That first week of school I was doe-eyed and very excited to get started to work, but not quite sure what I was getting myself into. The buildings and people looked very sophisticated and I felt less privileged compared to my classmates, as I was one of the few Latino students in most of my classes. I tried to brush the idea off that I did not belong at that school, but there were times when it was extremely difficult. Especially when I got handed my first final grades at that institution and received my first barely passing letter grade.

As an adult I returned to that small eight-year-old girl that felt very insecure. I questioned everything about me; I felt that the scholarship board had made a huge mistake by choosing me among other students that wanted to attend school. I felt that the seat I occupied in my classes could be filled by someone that needed it more than I did. I basically lost all the validation I had because I was always the smart sister and I no longer felt that I could be entitled to be that.

Then one of the worst things imaginable occurred, my brother passed away. I felt completely lost and my mental health that had been improving suddenly got worse. One of my unconditional supporters was no longer here for me. Then, I felt worse than I could have ever imagined. I felt like I had failed everyone in my life including myself because I was not feeling okay. I took two semesters off to take care of myself.

I came back in the spring semester and I have not dropped out since, the faith of God helped me understand that I used to get carried away and I did not listen to other opinions.

It has taken me years to realize that it is completely normal to have self-doubt. Although I am young, I have never once met someone that was sincerely confident in their lives. So, through the help of my family and religious leaders, I decided to once again talk to God and deliver my worries completely to him. It has been a very difficult journey to unlearn old habits that productiveness leads to success. I have begun to learn that we as humans need to take time to rest. At 23, I was extremely exhausted from all the demands my daily life entailed. I wanted to disappear from the face of this earth and I knew that I needed some time off from school for my well-being. Honestly, had I not taken time off from school I do not think that I would be here today, there was too much stress.

Mental health has become a part of my life and a priority for my well-being. Unfortunately, to this day it is not taken as seriously as it should be. I like to explain it this way: When we have a cold, we are recommended rest and sometimes prescribed medication. But, then why do people stigmatize mental health? Why are we being told just to, "Suck it up," or "There's people that have it way worse?" Then, there's people who just tell you, "It's all in your head!" Of course it is, it's in our brain—the most important and vital organ in our body.

As human beings, we will continue to have mental health battles that no one on this earth may be able to understand or see in their entirety, only God can. As a human being I have taken mental health medications, as well as sought the help of God and my loved ones, and no one should judge me for that. We do not live in a perfect world and I share my story because I want people to understand that mental health struggles can happen to anyone.

THIS IS ME

I am currently a senior getting a bachelor's degree in Paralegal Studies. I hold an associate's degree in Psychology. As a first generation student, I wish to share my story to inspire others to persevere regardless of consequences. I recently changed my faith to Christianity where I hold a closer relationship with God.

I dream of a future where I can help as many people as I can using my skills at the professional level as an advocate for the underrepresented community and as a fellow human being. I wish to remember my late brother Aldo by starting a nonprofit that focuses on youth programs that would enrich the lives of our youth in the community. When I am not studying, I spend most of my time reading, cooking, and spending time with my family. I give all glory to God for my achievements.

MY TEN-YEAR PLAN:

1. I wish to continue to grow my faith with God.
2. I want to be able to spend more time with my family.
3. I want to be able to be able to do missionary trips with my church.

LUCK = (HARD WORK) (OPPORTUNITIES)

DAYANA VILLAGRAN

"If I solely credit my luck, then I fail to validate my support system"

"What a lucky b---, she gets whatever she wants."

This thoughtless sentiment flooded me with anger and filled me with doubt. Why would someone feel this way towards me; why would someone say something in such a derogatory way; why would someone question what I had worked so hard for? Before this I had never questioned my accomplishments, but it was at this very moment that I began to question if I deserved all the blessings I had been granted and if I was even deserving of all the good things that came my way, or if there was someone more qualified and it was only by fluke that I took the prize.

I tried to justify this person's comment and attempted to answer why this person was questioning me. Perhaps things were happening too fast; maybe it was all the recognitions, scholarships, or internship job offers I had received due to my academic performance during my first years in college. I must admit the anger that flooded my thoughts emptied the doubt as quickly as it had filled my mind and since then I began to realize the number of times individuals have referred to me as being lucky.

Though it is easy to credit luck for the fulfillment of one's desires, luck is often the product of hard work and opportunities one sets up for themselves. It would be a foolish statement to diminish that which I have accomplished to mere luck, for I have earned the luck. If luck were a measurable quantification, it sure has come at a great cost—a cost I haven't been afraid to pay.

I was "lucky" enough to have put it upon myself to break the vicious cycle of being a migrant farm worker, to work countless hours in extreme weather conditions, not knowing the difference between sunrise from sunset and weekday from weekend since I was twelve years old. I was "lucky" enough to embark on the journey of restless nights of study, tormenting loneliness, and unaffordable failure during my undergraduate studies. I was "lucky" enough to earn a degree in a male dominated field where being dedicated equated to my stubbornness, where being passionate meant I was too emotional, and where being assertive depicted signs of aggression.

The rigor of the pursuit of an engineering degree allowed me to recognize that I will never be silenced nor give myself over to despondency and self-doubt. As a fire cannot begin or continue without sufficient oxygen; I have never allowed my candle to suffocate in the midst of adversity.

If I allow others' negative perception and conditional understanding of my character and let that define my achievements, I will feed into the idea that I have not worked for my accomplishments. Yet it is I who tirelessly continues to do whatever it takes to reach my goals. It is I who wakes up every morning willingly, and at times unwillingly, to overcome any obstacles thrown my way. Therefore, I cannot fail to validate myself because to discredit my hard work is to discredit the times when I felt like giving up but didn't allow myself to do so. There was something within me that didn't allow me to drown even when I couldn't swim. That something, or that someone, that disguised itself in courage and community, grit and gratitude, determination and obligation.

I have been told time and time again that I am a lucky individual. I only got chosen to represent the graduating class of Michigan State University for Fall 2021 because I was lucky; I only graduated debt free because I was lucky; I only got a full-time job offer from General Motors (GM) because I was lucky; I only got chosen to speak at the GM Latino Network Employee Resource Group because I was lucky. But even when others credit luck, I have come to the understanding that I have earned the right to be where I am and that I should allow myself to celebrate how far I have gotten, because my success is also a reflection of those who served as my support system. If I solely credit my luck, then I fail to validate my support system. I fail to validate my parents' countless counseling, my siblings' way of emboldening me, and my community's way of believing in me.

I cannot, in good faith, tell anyone that I will always feel confident and proud of my accomplishments, for at times I have felt defeated. I too, at times have felt a sense of failure that clouded my judgment, that shrouded my ability to appreciate the small wins. Yet I know I am not alone, because as humans, we tend to zero in on the lack of success rather than how a current and temporary state of failure is only a pit stop on the way to greater success. I can't guarantee that I will one day reach a sense of enlightenment through my personal journey of life, but I will say that I will never lose sight of my motivation, even if and as it changes, over time. I will always be working towards it, whatever it may be—whether it's my hopes, ambitions, self-fulfillment, or my own definition of success.

Like everything in life, I have a choice and I can choose to be proactive and shine in the light of progression, or to be reactive to the darkness of regression because as Michel De Montaigne stated, "He who fears he will suffer, already suffers because he fears." It is an ongoing battle to go from fearful to fearless, from powerless to powerful, and to lose the feeling of unworthiness for it is based on fallaciousness. For when the feeling of self-doubt roams my mind, I continuously task myself to give myself credit, detach from the situation, and view myself in the perspective that those who are proud of me would see me in. In the times that I have been my worst enemy, I must remind myself to be kind to myself and understand that I too was made for greatness.

Even in the moments when people aim to diminish my achievements and hard work, I reiterate that I have the power to stay strong, work hard, and believe in myself because I didn't get to where I am, nor will I get to where I want to be, just by being lucky.

THIS IS ME

My name is Dayana Villagran and I come from a migrant farm working family who has shown me to be proud of who I am and where I came from. I earned my bachelor's degree in Mechanical Engineering from Michigan State University and I work for General Motors at the Lansing Delta Township Assembly Plant under Central Engineering.

My main aspiration in life is to be able to help my family and give them a more pleasant lifestyle. I want to serve as evidence to my eight siblings that, with motivation, dedication, and hard work, anything is possible. I hope to express to others that education is a privilege that shouldn't be taken for granted. I will say, although I am young, I am hungry to learn, I am ambitious to succeed under my own definition of success, and I am grateful for the blessings I have been granted.

MY TEN-YEAR PLAN:

1. Personal: Buy a home where my parents and siblings can feel safe and welcomed.

2. Academic: Further my education by getting a master's in engineering or MBA to make myself more marketable and knowledgeable in the work field.

3. Professional: Serve in a position of leadership within General Motors.

DEJA QUE EL CORAZÓN Y TU COMUNIDAD SEAN TU GUÍA

ELIANNE "ELY" BAHENA

"Haz todo de corazón, porque cuando haces algo de corazón nunca puedes perder."

For as long as I can remember, I've had one passion—my community. I grew up in La Villita, or Little Village, a neighborhood on the Southwest side of Chicago, among immigrant families just like mine and where I built my community. This community cared for me, encouraged me, and helped raise me. My community gave me so much love as a child that, as a young adult, I couldn't help but to give that love back through my career.

My parents, Jesus and Modesta, are from Guerrero, Mexico. My dad is from Acapulco and my mom is from La Lagunita, a small pueblo with a population of 11 residents, right outside the town of Teloloapan. At 17 and 19 years old, my mom and dad migrated to the United States in search of opportunity and the promise of the American Dream.

As the eldest daughter to immigrant parents, I have carried the imaginary, but very real, weight of being the "first." Being the first to graduate high school, being the first to go to college, and being the first to navigate systems and pave the way for my family in the United States. As a first generation college student, failure wasn't ever an option, even as I struggled through school. After all, my parents had crossed rivers, mountains, and borders for me to have a future, and I had to convince myself that there was nothing I couldn't do compared to that. My time during college was often lonely and isolating but I kept going because I had a vision for my future, for my family, and for my community. In May of 2014, I became the first person in my family to graduate from college. This moment wasn't just for me but for my parents who had given their daughter everything even when they had nothing. Y ahora el mundo era mío.

As I began my job search, I saw an immigrant survivor advocate position at Mil Mujeres, a Latinx led national nonprofit organization that provided immigration legal services to survivors of domestic violence. As I read the job description, I knew in my heart that this was the perfect position for me.

I was ecstatic when I received a request for a first interview. I knew that this was where I wanted to be and I wanted to prove to them that I could do the work—there wouldn't be a fiercer advocate than me. During my second interview with the National Executive Director, she told me, "You should be very proud of yourself, it's between you and two other candidates." But, ultimately, I wasn't offered the position.

While I was disappointed, I went on and accepted a position at a private immigration law firm owned by a Latina lawyer, who operated an all women of color law firm. I jumped at the opportunity to work there, this was the first time I saw a Latina who looked like me, who had a career I could emulate—fighting for the rights of immigrant families.

Growing up, I didn't have a role model, but now as a young adult I had heroes like Justice Sonia Sotomayor, Dolores Huerta, Sandra Cisneros, and America Ferrera. They were women who looked like me, who were fearless and authentically themselves, and were breaking barriers. That's who I wanted to be.

My enthusiasm working at the law firm was short lived. I soon saw the toxic work environment we operated under. My "Latina Jefa" liked to belittle, chastise, and bully my fellow coworkers. She liked to pit us against each other and anything personal you shared about yourself could be used as her weapon. I didn't know what to do and I was tempted to quit but didn't know how it would affect my career. While speaking to my mom, she reminded me, "Haz todo de corazón, porque cuando haces algo de corazón nunca puedes perder." I loved the work I was doing, I loved working with the clients, and I loved who I was becoming. So I decided to stay in spite of knowing it was the wrong place for me.

During my time at the law firm, I took every opportunity to learn and I began to specialize in U-Visa, a form of immigration relief for survivors of domestic violence and other violent crimes in the United States, who had cooperated during their investigation. As I read police report after police report, I knew that the work I was doing wasn't enough—I wanted to understand how to be trauma informed and bring justice to survivors.

That's when I connected with Mujeres Latinas en Acción and I completed their sexual assault education and training, and applied to be a volunteer medical advocate in their sexual assault program. In my role, I provided support and information during the medical and criminal justice procedures to sexual assault survivors at four different hospitals in Chicago.

After almost a year with the law firm and now my volunteer work with Mujeres Latinas en Accion, I had no doubt that this was my passion. I wanted to advocate for immigrant survivors and I wanted to build stronger communities. I also made the decision that my time at the law firm had come to an end. I was walking away with knowledge, a passion, and a strong sense of who I wanted to be as Latina professional—one who leads with heart, justice, and kindness.

As I began my job search again, I saw a position open at Mil Mujeres, almost a year and half from when I first was rejected. Again, my heart guided me—it told me that's where I needed to be, that's where I could make the biggest impact for my community. I knew I could be rejected again, but like my mom says, cuando lo haces de corazón nunca puedes perder.

During my first interview, I was greeted once again by the National Executive Director, who asked with a smile, "Elianne, this is your second time applying for a position with us! What is it about us?"

This time around, I was offered the position. Later that year, I would go on to lead as the Director of the Chicago Chapter during the beginning of the Trump Administration. There would be many times during the next four years where I would feel lost and defeated, but my community and my heart always guided me back.

THIS IS ME

I am Elianne "Ely" Bahena, a proud daughter of immigrant parents from Guerrero, Mexico, a first-generation college graduate, and a passionate Latina leader from La Villita, who strives to empower and bring justice to my community. I have worked in the nonprofit sector for more than seven years, advocating for the protection of immigrant survivors of domestic violence and for the rights of immigrant communities across Illinois. This year, I began a new position at the 22nd Ward Public Service Office, where I serve as the Director of Policy and Community Outreach.

I am on the Board of Directors of Mujeres Latinas en Accion after leading their Young Professional Advisory Council as Chairwoman in 2020, and being a volunteer with the organization since 2015. I am the Chairwoman of Enlace Chicago's Associate Board (ECAB), an Executive Board member in the HACE Chicago Auxiliary Board, and the Co-Chair of the Young Women's Giving Council at the Chicago Foundation for Women.

I am a Trabajadoras Fellow with the Labor Council for Latin American Advancement and part of the inaugural class for Community Leadership Fellows.

MY TEN-YEAR PLAN:

1. Graduate from law school and expand existing legal clinics/programs in Little Village.

2. Continue to write—my mom has asked me to help her write her story.

3. Embrace joy and travel, every opportunity I have! Japan is next on my list!

EMBRACE WHO YOU ARE

JAZMIN VALDERRAMA

"Be proud of who you are today and where you came from yesterday."

YOUNG AND NAÏVE

Like many young Latinos who are products of immigrants, I was raised speaking mostly Spanish at home and English at school. I read, write, and think in two languages and I value morals from both cultures. I am a beautiful and complicated mix. A proud American and even prouder Latina. Yet, I struggled fitting within the box of one culture or the other.

"Where are you from?" A frequent question I was asked growing up in New York City, where you can find immigrants from almost every country in the world.

"Me? I'm from Colombia." This was the answer I always led with. I don't have any recollection of anyone ever teaching me what the best response was. For as long as I can remember, I have always been: *Colombiana, porque mi sangre es del Valle de Cauca.*

I was challenged from time to time: "Well, if you were born in the United States, you are American."

I remember feeling the blood rush to my face. *I am NOT an American.*

For a long time, I despised the thought of being categorized as an American. I was young and naïve. In my mind, an American was an average Joe from the suburbs of Middle America. I grew up in a city—the best city. Filled with people of all colors and ethnicities. I felt that I was more than American, I was a New Yorker.

Looking back, my preconceived notions around what it meant to be an American definitely hindered me. I grew up with a passionate Colombian mother, who always said she came into this world being three things: Colombian, Catholic and a salsa lover—and that is how she will go out.

I had an appreciation for the people, food, music, and unique traits of being Latino in the US and growing up in Queens, NY—one of the most diverse cities in the world—helped feed the pride I had of being a Latina.

FEELING THE PRESSURE

While I had all this pride in my youth, as I approached adulthood, I was always hesitant to show my Latina side around non-Latinos. I felt the pressure to conform and limit the very things that made me, well me. A little emphasis on certain words here and there to somewhat hide a small accent I had naturally when speaking English. Changing my demeanor to be a little less passionate, a bit more neutral. I would order food from fellow Latinos at the deli and I would speak in English. There was always a bit of awkwardness in the air since it was apparent that I had some sort of Latina roots in me.

I look back and think how sad it must have been for these hard-working immigrants to finally see someone of their kind walk into their place of work, feeling a sense of similarity, only to be disappointed by the lack of friendliness and the hindrance of getting an order in a language that would've made everything so much easier.

Fast forward to my twenties, I felt like I was intentionally whitewashing myself once I entered the corporate world. With each passing day, I lost a bit of fluency in speaking Spanish. I found myself struggling to find words when talking to Spanish speaking family members.

At the same time, I felt myself grow intellectually and culturally (learning about non-Latino cultures). I pushed past several limiting beliefs, self-doubt, and insecurities. I struggled not having a Latino/a role model in my life to show it was possible to make it in Corporate America.

FINDING MY PEOPLE

I was longing for a common ground in all aspects of my life. Then, in what seemed like some sort of divine intervention from a higher power, I came across a role—my dream role really—at one of the biggest US Spanish language media companies. It was in that moment that I realized, I was now hesitant that I *wasn't Latina enough* to work at this company. It was a huge turning point for me—personally and professionally.

The interview process was seamless. The team I would eventually be on was full of strong, confident, powerful Latinas who were fluent in both languages, identified with both cultures, and made it look easy. Up until that point, I never thought this existed. A new world that seemed made for people like me. I will never forget the wave of emotions I felt when I received the job offer.

My mom, who never really paid mind to where exactly I was working—as long as I was using my degree somewhere—came to tears when I gave her the news. She bought me a cake the night before my first day. It felt like a full circle moment—this was destiny.

Over the next two years I grew to sharpen my mental agility tremendously. Emailing in Spanish, having meetings in Spanglish, and sharing so many common experiences with coworkers. I pushed past a lot of emotional trauma that was engrained in my mind and shifted my mindset from feeling grateful for everything I have by realizing that I was worthy of my accomplishments. I too deserved a seat at the table, no matter if my upbringing and education was different from those around me. I was finally proud of what I had done and, on the contrary, I wanted MORE.

To top it off, I was assigned to work on a brand that communicated these nuanced experiences of bilingual, bicultural Latinos in the US—Just. Like. Me. Not only did I find people like me, I learned so much about other Latin American and Caribbean countries. I learned just how similar all Latinos are.

I learned about the history that brought us to be who we are, brought us the music we adore today, and so much more.

The moral of the story here is follow your gut and embrace your uniqueness . Be proud of who you are today and where you came from yesterday. You are in control of your own identity, own it.

THIS IS ME

My name is Jazmin Valderrama. I am a born and bred New Yorker with roots from Colombia. Naturally, I am a go-getter with an "I can do it all" mindset. I am a passionate brand marketer currently working for one of the largest advertising agencies in the world. I have by far surpassed my wildest expectations and hope to be a role model for up and coming talent within the workforce. I am just as humble as I am tenacious. I am my own inspiration.

MY TEN-YEAR PLAN:

1. Diversify my portfolio across different areas of income.

2. Travel to cities that are actually NOT on my bucket list and be open to new and different experiences.

3. Find a true sense of balance in my life when it comes to work, family, friends, academic growth, creating my home, and, most importantly, having me time.

ELIZABETH MARQUEZ

"Si te dicen que no lo puedes hacer, enséñales que si"

Growing up I didn't have much control over the direction of my life. I was told to go to school, get good grades, and get a good job. As a good Mexican daughter of immigrant parents, I did as I was told. I graduated high school early and did the "smart" money saving thing and went to community college to start. I decided I wanted to study to be a nurse. I took one human anatomy class and, even though I excelled in the one I took in high school, I failed at this one. I felt lost. High school was so easy for me and now I was failing all my classes? What was wrong with me?

About a year in, I found out I was expecting a child with my boyfriend. This was not part of the plan. I was supposed to graduate college and be the first person in my family to do so. Getting pregnant, this is not what a good daughter does. I hid my pregnancy as long as I could while making a plan to escape the wrath of my parents. The first person I told was my older sister. I thought that she could help ease the blow when I told my father. He was the one I was more worried about disappointing. He thought so highly of me and was so proud that I was going to college he bought me a brand new car my senior year of high school so I could go to work.

I brought a picture of my ultrasound and put it in a little box I bought at the dollar store. Filled it with confetti and crinkled cut paper. Told him it was a late birthday present. I started recording to capture the beautiful moment when he knew he would be a grandpa for the first time. He opened it up confused, looked at my sister and said, "Are you expecting?" My sister was seven years older than me with a long term partner so it was safe to assume that she was the one with the baby. She shook her head no and you could instantly see his face change.

He stayed quiet for what seemed like an eternity. Then started asking questions at a rapid pace: "Who's the father? What will you do for money? When is the baby due? Where will you live? What do you plan to do with school?" Before I answered anything he said, "You're not going to end up doing anything with your life." I was in disbelief. He didn't yell at me, but the words he uttered hurt more. I would have preferred the yelling.

I eventually left community college while being on academic probation. I worked at a restaurant when I was pregnant. There was a server who was in his 60's, who had lived in Mexico for many years. I asked him about Mexico and how his life was there. He said the place he loved the most was Playa del Carmen. I googled it and thought I would be lucky to ever visit that place, especially now that money was so tight.

I had my daughter when I was just 19 years old. I fought post-partum depression for a year. My partner didn't understand post-partum depression and I didn't blame him since he was only 20. We separated. I was heartbroken.

One day I stared into my daughter's eyes and realized that I could do better. I wanted to give her a life that was truly better than mine. I had to reapply to community college and worked full-time. I was accepted to DePaul University, then transitioned to working part-time while taking a full course load. I landed a couple of internships and eventually secured a full-time job as a tax associate at a public accounting firm my junior year of college.

In 2020 the pandemic started. I had to navigate taking a full course load while also teaching my kindergartener from home. I reconciled my romantic relationship with my daughter's father, but that brought along its own challenges. I wore many hats throughout the years—mother, daughter, wife, and student. The question was, who was Elizabeth?

I graduated in the spring of 2021 and Ariana, my daughter, graduated kindergarten as well. We did it. Shortly after her father and I separated for a final time. I started off 2022 working many hours raising a six year old child and a puppy. I didn't expect to be doing this alone. Then again, I didn't expect many things that occurred in my life.

When we are going through a difficult time, we forget that after every struggle or challenge there is happiness or a lesson that comes with it. In 2022, although the life that I had planned for myself completely changed, I remembered that my life also changed when I was 19. If I could do that, I can also work through the feeling of being lost. I decided to focus on finding myself again. The past few years I was so focused on everyone else in my life that I forgot about myself. Now, here I am at 26 writing this while sitting on the beach of Playa del Carmen on vacation.

Things don't go the way you plan sometimes and that is okay. As long as you take the chance to make what you want yours, nothing can stop you. For some people a degree is just a piece of paper, but for me it gave me an opportunity to give my daughter a better life. It gave me the opportunity to discover who I am again. To everyone who has doubts about your abilities, to everyone who thinks they are too old to start something or feel like it's too late to finish something, you'll be surprised at what you can achieve. Don't give up on yourself because others don't see your potential.

THIS IS ME

My name is Elizabeth and I am the first person in my family to graduate college. I am a tax associate at a public accounting firm. I want to learn about the business world and how to help others. Eventually I would love to transition to working for a non-profit because I want to use my knowledge and expertise to make a difference in the world. After gaining more experience I hope to have my own non-profit organization.

MY TEN-YEAR PLAN:

1. Travel the world with my daughter.

2. Start my own non-profit organization.

3. Provide my family with new life experiences.

BALANCING IT ALL

CYNTHIA PADILLA

"Learn your value. Lean on those that believe and support you and find ways to advocate for your needs—all of them."

"How do you balance it all?" I am often asked when I talk about being a full-time professional, mamá, and graduate student. My response is usually, "I cry. A lot." And it is half true. Early on, there were many days that I would be frantically working on assignments to meet a deadline while my older daughter, Julia, slept on me. When Elena was born, summer 2021, I cried while I was feeding her right before my dissertation proposal defense and after my presentation because I was so exhausted and glad for that stage to be over. Arriving to this point, where I was actively doing tasks for three roles, was a decision that I did not make lightly.

Growing up, my dad always instilled the importance of education to me, my brother, and sister. He taught us about diversity, feminism, and being proud of our Mexican culture long before we knew how this would impact our lives. You see, we grew up on the southside of Chicago and moved to the suburbs when I was nine years old. Talk about a culture shift—going from having a lot of diversity in my classes to experiencing a lack of diversity throughout high school. Later, learning that the lack of diversity would be the case throughout my college experience.

Fast forward to college, I knew I wanted to work in education. Educational Psychology was the road for me to get there because of the focus on how people learn and the research opportunities. I went to College of Lake County, transferred to Northeastern Illinois University studied Psychology, and earned my master's from Northern Illinois University in Educational Psychology. Throughout these educational milestones, I was always working in retail, serving, and on grant funded positions. Working on grants is where I realized that I enjoyed working with students to learn about and plan for college.

My first job after earning my master's degree was working in the TRIO-Student Support Services (TRIO-SSS) program at the College of Lake County (CLC). Although this position entailed a lot of emotional labor because of the close relationships I formed with students, I always enjoyed it. When the opportunity opened for the project director role, I applied and was offered the position. This is where I grew the most in my leadership and management style.

PLANNING FOR GRADUATE WORK AS A MAMÁ

I knew that I wanted to earn my doctorate degree and that there is never a perfect time to start a program. I always had an issue with the statistics of Latina doctorate degree earners because the need to have representation in academia and in research are necessary in order to make real change. I enjoy learning and knew that graduate work could push me to think more critically about higher education. I had a supportive supervisor, Eric, and Dean, Tanya, and they continue to be the examples of leadership that I want to be and adapt. These relationships, especially with Eric, were important deciding factors in applying to a doctoral program. His leadership and support made balancing my work responsibilities and coursework easy which was logistically important.

As a parent, I asked two colleagues about their experiences. Tanya was in a doctorate program and her children were older—in high school and planning for college. Ali, completed her doctorate program when her child was little. After hearing their experiences, I realized that I wanted to pursue my doctorate degree while Julia was small and I had family that I could lean on. Julia was one year old when I started my doctorate degree. When I started the program, I was able to easily read and complete assignments after Julia fell asleep. Or, work on assignments while Julia played independently.

TAKING BACK CONTROL OF MY LIFE
Postpartum kicked my butt! I was pregnant with Elena (2020-2021) during my last two semesters of coursework and she was born before my last summer semester of coursework and the beginning of dissertating. When Elena was born,

having two children and planning writing time seemed like an impossible task. While I was on parental leave from work, there was a point where I no longer recognized myself. The feelings I remember were the weight of stress and anxiety, like the sensation of drowning. I lost myself. I felt so numb. What saved my life was making the decision to work with a therapist and my primary physician. I learned that I was struggling with maybe anxiety, maybe postpartum depression, and baby blues, along with balancing other responsibilities.

Through therapy, I found my voice again and made critical life-decisions. This was particularly frightening because I realized that I was going to jeopardize ending many relationships and, yet, this risk was crucial for my well-being. The difficult part of my experience was the internal dissonance of feeling of great sadness and the guilt of not being with my littles as often as I wanted, while knowing that I wanted and chose to be in this experience at this moment of my life. I wish I would have made this decision sooner. Due to my postpartum experience, I do not remember the first four or five months of Elena's life or how I even did life while having two kids, returning to work, and moving forward with my dissertation.

In reflecting on my experience, I realized that I was not the best at voicing the need for someone to help play with my girls while I worked on my coursework and writing. My mom recognized this and on several occasions she would often invite herself to spend time with Julia and Elena so that I could complete assignments and keep along with my writing timeline for my dissertation. I wish I would have leaned more on my mom, family members, and friends to help with my girls. I would have been less stressed and overwhelmed through this process.

While it may seem impossible to be a mamá, professional, and advance professionally or through education while balancing life, there is always a way. Learn your value. Lean on those that believe and support you and find ways to advocate for your needs—all of them. For this reason, I am transparent about my experiences, so that other women can learn through me, prepare for their own success, and know that they are not alone.

THIS IS ME

I am Cynthia Padilla. I am the mamá of two beautiful littles, Julia and Elena. I work at the College of Lake County as the Manager of Student Success Strategy, where I assist on college-wide student success initiatives and projects. I recently completed an Ed.D in Higher Education specializing in Community College Leadership from Northern Illinois University.

My dream for the future is to impact the lives of Latinx employees working in higher education. My dissertation research focused on the Leadership of Latina women working in community college and extending this topic to include Latinx employees in academia is important. I intend to publish my dissertation and present at conferences across the country.

MY TEN-YEAR PLAN:

1. Engage with and conduct research on leadership in higher education and with Latina women and Latinx employees.

2. Travel, anywhere, domestically and internationally, with my siblings, mom, a few solo trips, and with my littles.

3. Continue learning about personal finance to help me continue to be financially independent and build generational wealth.

TIME IS ON NO ONE'S SIDE

ALEXANDRA TURCIOS

"Being young—there is the impression of having the good fortune of time on your side. That couldn't be farther from the truth."

It is mid-day on a bright summer day in June. I am sitting at my desk preparing for my next meeting. For me, the moments of in-between are held in high regard. This pause, this momentary respite—it is what calibrates me. The clock, however, ticks, glimmering with a golden aura, as if it's the center of the universe and commands my attention. I hone in on its hand slowly moving around its circular façade not knowing what to expect. In a few minutes, I'll be speaking with an Executive Director of a large Chicago-based institution.

TICK. TOCK. TICK. TOCK.

These calls are normal, but my pulse is palpable, echoing the tick of the clock perked up on my desk reminding me, again, that time is a finite resource. I must focus. I must execute. I must get it all done. Enter my mind and you'll soon realize it's a labyrinth that winds like an infinite staircase. Each level unlocks a new goal, ambition, and put simply—there is not enough time.

Perhaps that is why I am persistently on the go. The constant ticking of the clock reverberates in my mind even when I'm away from my desk. Being young—there is the impression of having the good fortune of time on your side. That couldn't be farther from the truth. What a myth that is—perhaps one of a myriad of hidden superpowers and acts of deception you can get away with. For example: you are young and naïve, when in reality, you hold a wealth of wisdom—more than others presume. You are organized and professional, when in reality, it's a veneer you show the world to cover the chaos of jam-packed days filled with complex agendas because you want to stretch yourself more and more like a compulsion you must give into. You have time on your side, when, time is finite for us all and the pressure to perform and seize every moment is almost unbearable.

Did you know, the average human life span is about 4,000 weeks? Each passing moment is a reminder of that abysmal fate. The sense of urgency to reach goals and milestones and being cognizant of the limitation time poses, is perhaps my greatest motivator. It is also why the moments of in-between, of pause between heart beats, makes me feel alive. I intentionally feel the empty space before every meeting: small or big. I never know how these dialogues will pan out—what the other person is thinking. Will they be pleasant? Will they question my ability? Are there pre-conceived notions interlaced with that person's own projections and insecurities?

The call I am about to have with an Executive Director: this is considered normal. For years, I've been a young leader who relishes in the opportunity to set a vision and execute on it. I am currently at the helm of the largest Auxiliary Board for a Latino-serving non-profit in Chicago where I lead a group of 20 individuals on a mission to being the #1 Latino/a/x serving Auxiliary Board in Chicago. It's a lofty yet tangible goal that we've been able to deconstruct and execute against. Outside of this pro bono work, I have worked in the Management Consultant and Strategy space for the past seven years providing cutting-edge innovation, frameworks, and technology implementation for a variety of Fortune 100 companies. It's not the other person's role, their carefully refined persona, or their status, that gives me an adrenaline rush—but the social anxiety that accompanies these first encounters.

It's time to join the call and before me flashes the video screen with her posing, deliberately and intentionally. She sits tall in her chair, in a posture that has been carefully defined over years of fighting for—and maintaining—a seat at the table. Behind her is a built-in bookcase made of walnut wood, displaying an array of awards, certifications, and trinkets collected from exotic locations. She flashes a large smile as she greets me. I feel my lips curve upward to reveal a soft smile. We exchange niceties and she introduces her entry-level coordinator, Emilie, who assists with notetaking and other meeting logistics. Before allotted the opportunity to drive our agenda, the E.D. blurts out a comment that catches me off guard:

"You're so young. Wow—look, Emilie, anything is truly possible!"

In that moment, I was stumped. A rush of emotions swells the cavity of my chest, and I remember the source of the anxiety around conducting business as a young, ambitious Latina. In that moment, I was reduced to my appearance, my perceived age, despite having a decade worth of work experience under my belt.

My response in my mind is: "Absolutely! Anything [that you put countless hours, training, dedication, natural talent, and passion into] is possible!" What is possible is defying stereotypes or boxes others try to put you in.

Instead, feeling paralyzed, I chuckle and proceed to my presentation.

It doesn't matter that by the end the E.D. confesses: "I understand why you are in your position. You are a very strong leader."

The meeting is suddenly over—it feels like a relief. I feel content I could dissipate doubt by delivering value. Yet, this concept of time returns to my mind.

My attention returns to the tick of the clock, its iridescent glow reminds me of how precious time is for us all. Time is on no one's side. It is what we do with moments of disruption, of doubt, of misconceptions, and how we decide to use it to fortify our inner strength. Time is not on your side if you are not resilient and able to bounce back from difficulties. The only guarantee is your own ownership over emotion, over deciding your outlook, and if you will let others perception of you get in the way of

executing on goals. That is why these moments of in-between—
the ticks of the clock—are held in such high regard. To ground
myself in the present moment, lean into my inner stillness, and
march courageously toward breaking more barriers.

THIS IS ME

My name is Alexandra Turcios. I am a proud daughter of Honduran immigrants who left their native country to provide greater opportunities to me and my four siblings. Their sacrifice was not in vain and opened pathways to become the first - but certainly not the last. I am part of the 2% of Latinas who work in a STEM field and currently work as a Strategic & Technical Consultant for Adobe. I am passionate about the disparity in the workplace as it relates to Latino representation and in my free time, I serve as the Chairwoman of the Chicago Chapter of the Hispanic Alliance for Career Enhancement (the largest HACE auxiliary chapter nationally) where I lead a team of 20 individuals on the mission to cultivate career changing programming and opportunities for the 80,000+ members of HACE. This tireless work earned me two 40 Under 40 awards from Negocios Now and HACE. Additional philanthropic work includes serving on the Board of Directors at the Tree House Humane Society, an animal welfare non-profit in Chicago.

I graduated in the top 3% of my class at the University of Illinois at Urbana-Champaign where I was named a "Bronze Scholar" and was later recognized as a prestigious Fulbright Scholar to serve as an ambassador of the U.S. Department of State in Indonesia. I returned to my alma mater in 2022 to pursue an MBA with a focus on Entrepreneurship & Strategic Innovation and Digital Marketing.

I have worked with some of the top brands and companies of the world - many in the Fortune 100 and dream of serving on a Corporate Board of Directors to add to the 1% of Latinas who currently have a seat at the table. In addition to this aspiration, I want to one day become an Angel Investor to identify, foster, and scale Latino innovation.

MY TEN-YEAR PLAN:

1. Rise to a Director level role at my respective company and standardize on embedding more inclusion and diversity of hiring practices

2. Become an Angel Investor to identify, foster, and scale Latino innovation

3. Take calculated risks: start and scale my own entity (non-profit or company)

MARIELA ESQUIVEL-RODRIGUEZ

"Our parents' strengths have to outweigh their weaknesses."

MY MOMENT

Unforgettable tears came down my face as I hugged my papi, feeling the tears from his fall onto my shirt. He hugged me tight, and without saying any words, I knew that he was proud of me. This is how our immigrant parents tell us they love us, and we show them we love them by proving that their sacrifice of moving to a new country was worth it.

In the spring of 2022, I was invited to participate in a scholarship luncheon—the theme was first-generation college students. I got asked to be a part of a video and speak at the luncheon on a panel, and this was a special moment for me in my college career. I called my papi on the phone, asking him to please try to make it to the luncheon during his break. "Déjame ver lo que puedo hacer mija... invita mejor a tu mami, yo ni entiendo ingles para que voy."

My heart fell to my feet. It hurt me that my own dad couldn't feel welcomed to a special event for me because he didn't understand the language. "No importa esta bien por favor no mas puedes venir?" My mami already told me she wouldn't be able to come because of work, so my two guests that had name tags waiting for them at the luncheon were my dad and my older sister.

When they arrived, my dad was in a rush outside changing from his dirty work clothes and boots into jeans, a collared shirt, and his Mexico cap. He right away felt out of place after seeing the setup and how everyone else was dressed, but I knew that no one else belonged to be there more than him.

I was asked the question for the panel, *"What will your degree mean to you and represent for your entire family?"*

As I responded, I mentioned that this degree isn't just for me, it is also for my parents and for their sacrifices of hard work. This degree that I am working for is a representation of new opportunities and a leap of faith. It's my parents' leap of faith to come to a new country, and a leap of faith to be the first one to move out from home and attend college. I then took the time to translate this into Spanish—even if my dad was the only non-English speaker in the room, I made sure that he would understand. My dad was in tears, making it hard to even look over at him.

After the panelists each answered a question, we were surprised and awarded a two-thousand-dollar scholarship. I had no idea this was happening, and I was so grateful. This proves that just by sharing our stories, big things will come from them. I walked back down to hug my dad and kissed his cheek, knowing that if he didn't emphasize the importance of education at home, I wouldn't be where I am today.

FAMILY

Experiences like this didn't happen all the time at home, and that's why I hold that memory with me so closely. Life at home growing up wasn't easy as a low-income, daughter of immigrants. Homework was difficult to do sometimes because of the language, but I never blamed my parents for not knowing how to help me with schoolwork. I knew they didn't understand English much, so from an early age I had to learn to do it on my own. I interpreted field trip permission slips, important documents, and checked off my work. I was young, but was expected to get good grades, never get into trouble, and complete all my homework.

PATIENCE

After finishing my first semester at Northwest Nazarene University (NNU), I was in a state of mind where I have never wanted to give up so badly. I pushed myself so hard and wanted to be the best and create change on my campus right when I stepped foot there.

One night, I was on the phone with my former TRIO Upward Bound specialist, Josh Engler. "This isn't fair! Why do they have it so easy?" I wished my parents were able to help me in the same way my peers did. "I can't do this anymore!" I sobbed.

"You've lost yourself. But you need to give it another chance.

Let me tell you something, it is never going to get easier," he told me. "Breathe in, breathe out."

"Yea, I know, but okay I'll try." I responded, wiping my tears with my sleeve. I stared up at the stars in the sky and thought to myself, *Mami and Papi, forgive me for being so angry that you cannot help me.* I felt so much guilt for even thinking that I wished my parents could just know more and that I wasn't a first-generation student. One more chance.

GROWTH

I looked forward to the new semester because each semester is a fresh start. The second semester, I took things slow. I focused more on my grades, but kept sharing my story. When I did this, doors were opened to new opportunities.

I was hurt and angry that my parents didn't know enough to help me through college, but I have learned that these experiences as first-generation college students are what shape us, make us stronger, and make us grateful. My parents left everything they had in Mexico to come to a new country, to work, and provide new opportunities for their family. We sometimes might not agree with the traditional Mexican mindsets they used to raise us, but how can they know any better? Growing up in Mexico is all they knew, and they raised their children here in the US the same.

I used to get so angry that this is how they parented us, but I am learning it was not their fault, just their experiences. And sometimes, we must think about all the goodness our parents have given us. As a mentor of mine, Maria Gonzalez, once told me, "Our parents' strengths have to outweigh their weaknesses."

My parents gifted me with a beautiful culture that has delicious food, vibrant colors, beautiful dancing, and the ambition to always work hard and care for la familia. They gifted me with a language that I use to communicate with them. Where they smile at me when I roll my R's, speak fast, and even mispronounce words. They gifted me with a beautiful name that, with time, I have taught people to say my name the way they say it. With a hard rolled R, and the soft A at the end. They've gifted me with a roof over my head, food at the table, and most importantly access to new opportunities than what they were ever given.

To my mami and papi, thank you for coming with nothing, but being able to give me everything.

THIS IS ME

My name is Mariela Esquivel-Rodriguez, and I am currently 20 years old, entering junior year as a first-generation college student at Northwest Nazarene University. I am the daughter of immigrants to mis papis Raul Esquivel and Irma Rodriguez, a younger sister to one of my many role models, Esmeralda, and an older sister to Noelia and Diego.

At NNU I am majoring in social work and minoring in professional writing, in hopes to start my own non-profit one day. I am passionate about representation in my community, advocating for the unheard, and empowering the young generation of Latinos around me. I want to be a woman who creates changes, touches lives, and continues to live the dream of my mami and papi who helped me spread my wings for me to fly.

I want to be the director of my own non-profit organization that'll change and inspire many lives of underrepresented Latinos in Idaho and eventually around the world.

MY TEN-YEAR PLAN:

1. Intern for the Congressional Hispanic Caucus Institute in Washington, D.C.
2. Get into graduate school to get my master's in social work and non-profit management
3. Marry the love of my life and work together to successfully create change together for underrepresented communities.

LORENA GUDINO

"To be able at any moment, to sacrifice what you are, for what you will become." – Eric Thomas

Around age six I vividly remember being woken up in the middle of the night and being taken to my cousin's house to have my first sleepover. In my household it was a very known thing that sleepovers were not allowed at all. The whole night I knew something was wrong, my Hispanic parents were letting me have a sleepover. Not knowing why I was having a sleepover in the middle of the night is what made me stay up the whole night. It is a weird feeling to describe, but I knew something was off that night. As time went on, I soon realized that things were going to change.

From that night forward I saw my mother less and less. This caused my dad to sit me down on the couch and explain to me what cancer was and how it was damaging my mom. My mom had a few surgeries done and was soon having to go through chemo and radiation therapy to try to stop the cancer from spreading. My mom had stage 2 cancer, close to stage 3, but she never stopped fighting. Against everything she continued to get her treatments and surgeries.

I went to go see my mom after a few weeks of her being in the hospital, the image of first seeing my mom at her lowest still sticks with me. It's an image I can't get out of my head. The part that I always remember is that when I walked through the door she welcomed me with open arms. No matter how sick my mom got she always had her arms open for me to hug her. No matter how tired or nauseous she felt, she was always there.

My mom and I don't exactly see eye to eye on a lot of things, but I know that she will never push me away when I need her. That's what I love the most about her, something she always tells me is: "Yo meto mis manos al fuego por ti." Which is, "I'll always stick my hands in the fire for you."

She will always defend me and have my best interest. As I've grown up, I've slowly learned what that phrase means. Sadly, because my mom was still not let out of the hospital, my dad and grandma, from my mom's side, thought it would be best for her to come to the United States and help take care of all of us.

When my grandma on my mom's side came for the first time, I had never felt such instant love for a person I just met— she was truly a ray of pure joy. She made everyone around her smile. I am forever grateful to her for helping me through those rough and confusing times. Once my mom was finally able to come home I felt this sense of relief and my stress finally calmed down.

One vivid memory I have is when my mom shaved her hair—I saw my beautiful mother doubt her beauty because her hair had been shaved off. I told her everyday she was beautiful no matter what and I hope she knows I meant it from the bottom of my heart.

My mom, this December of 2022, will be declared NEC (no evidence of cancer) for 10 years. My mom is a survivor not just of cancer, but of so many things in life. Things I know I wouldn't be able to go through without her. I love her more than my life. Even the days we get mad at each other—at the end of the day we hold each other through the hard times.

My grandma from my mom's side passed away from stomach cancer, a very painful and slow cancer. Having to say goodbye over the phone is something that still upsets me. The fact that I couldn't hold her once more to say how much I loved her and how she saved me at such a young age. I know it was hard on my mom; it's still hard on the both of us.

My mom was also there to hold me when my grandma from my dad's side passed away. I was in school and didn't know until my mom told me the tragic news. It's such a weird feeling to feel your stomach sink as your brain processes the news. My grandma died of liver cancer, another painful cancer.

These three women have made me into the person I am. Even through heartache they have been the most influential people in my life. They have taught me so many valuable lessons that they impact my life to this day.

I never really stopped to think about how my mom's

sickness really affected me, but now that I'm older I've begun to really analyze it. There were negative and positive affects seeing my mom fighting and not giving up regardless of how terrible it really got, which inspires me to this day. It is something I always remind myself of. It made me mature quicker—whether that is seen as a good or bad thing is up for discussion.

Something that's definitely on the negative side is how anxious I get with my mom. If she takes too long when she goes anywhere, I start to panic and worry that something might go wrong. My mom recently had another major surgery a few months ago, during the entire time of her surgery I couldn't eat. My stomach locks up and I can't eat food.

Through this, I also learned quality over quantity. I have a handful of friends that I know will always be there for me no matter what. I don't tell a lot of people about my mom or about her cancer. I have noticed I don't trust people easily. I find that I'd rather be by myself, than get up and meet new people. It makes me anxious.

Losing both my grandmas to cancer has impacted me greatly. Seeing the people I love the most go through so much pain really makes me thankful to have them in my life—or to have had them. I'm even more thankful that my mom has become a survivor of cancer. I know not everyone beats that battle. I truly never got to thank my grandmas for all they did for me. My grandmas played a tremendous part in helping me become the person I am. My heart goes out to every person that either has cancer or has someone close to them with cancer.

THIS IS ME

I'm Lorena Gudino; my Dad is from Mexico and my Mom is from Peru. I am described as a wise, caring, and genuine person. Right now I am a senior in high school and will be continuing to go to school after I graduate. My mom always tells me how important school is and I believe her. I don't know exactly what I want to pursue just yet, but I do know I want to help people. I want to be able to make a difference in people's lives, not just my own. My parents came from nothing to a new country, not knowing the language, having to discover how this country works. The opportunities I've been given aren't something I'm going to take for granted. I'm going to make my parents proud, but most importantly I'm going to make myself proud.

I love my friends and my family that have always supported me—my parents giving me the most support I could ever ask for. It's something I don't always thank them for, but I truly do thank God that I have the parents that I do. Even if my mom and I don't see eye to eye on a lot of things, I know she's always going to protect me—I know she's always willing to put her hands in the fire for me. I'm not usually a person that opens up about my mom's story to just anyone, but she is my rock. *Mis padres son la bendición más grande de mi mundo, por el esfuerzo de ellos yo tengo las oportunidades que yo tengo en este país.*

MY TEN-YEAR PLAN:

1. Have my own company and become CEO.

2. Have my own house.

3. Be finished with school and complete my Masters.

THE JOURNEY TO OVERCOMING A NIGHTMARE

NATALIA RAMIREZ

"Do not be afraid to speak up."

We all have moments in our life that mark us forever. While they can be positive or negative, they have the power to affect your life 100 percent. I am sharing my story today, to speak my truth and with the hopes that it can inspire others who are going through something similar.

My family is originally from Colombia. Both my parents were born there and most of my extended family is still there. They immigrated to the US together and my brother and myself were born here. My family is one of many that moved to the US in search for a better life. My parents growing up worked hard—often in minimum wage jobs—to provide for us. I always admired them as they worked hard, but stayed positive despite the challenges they faced—language barriers, lack of education, not the best work conditions and other obstacles. As children of immigrants, we often see our parents sacrifice so much for us. Growing up I always saw this and tried to be a well behaved child and make my parents proud.

My parents worked hard to give my brother and me an education and opportunities. Of course, this didn't prevent me from also facing some challenges of my own. In late elementary school I suffered from bullying and horrible harassment from boy classmates as my body was developing. Unfortunately, my teacher did not act appropriately and blamed me for provoking this unwanted attention. I never told my parents about this nor did I want to make it a big deal because I knew they had tons of things going on and my problems seemed like they weren't enough to speak up about. Looking back, I wish I could have shared this with my family and know how important it is to speak up about uncomfortable situations.

This took a toll on me and I became more antisocial and kept to myself. I had friends and played soccer, but I could feel how this internally affected me. What came next was something I was not prepared for. During the summer of my sophomore year, I was hanging out with a childhood friend who had invited me to his house to catch up and say hello to his mom. However, as we arrived no one was there. I was concerned that he lied to me and as I finished that thought, he locked the door and I became frightened. He was much bigger than me he grabbed me and took me to his room. I was sexually assaulted and raped. I hid and kept this a secret for months.

This traumatic experience affected me in every part of my life. I was scared, ashamed, and felt alone as I told no one. Once school started, seeing boys in the hallway would frighten me. I was not able to stand beside a boy without being afraid they were going to do something to me. I felt like no one would understand me. I could not take a break from the thoughts running through my head and would get anxiety attacks in school. I remember asking for permission to go to the bathroom and trapping myself in a stall crying—not being able to breathe, trembling, feeling like I was getting trapped in a black hole.

At home it wasn't much better. Not even going to sleep was an escape. I would wake up all the time sweating and bursting into tears. I would get sleep paralysis every day and I was trapped in the same nightmare as I had experienced. Now I know that I was experiencing was PTSD (Post-Traumatic Stress Disorder).

I am sad to say that for months I suffered alone. Despite me interacting with my family, I decided to stay quiet about this. My dad would pick me up from school and we would talk normally in the car. We'd pick up my mom from work and go home. We'd have dinner and my parents would go to sleep early to go to work the next day. I knew how important it was for them to work and I felt like I didn't want to add a burden to them. I did not want them to stop working or have them take days off to deal with me. I was hurting, but acted as if nothing had happened.

Eventually, the emotional trauma I was dealing with became too much and I decided to speak up. My mom found me crying one day in my room and decided enough was enough. It was one of the hardest things I have had to do, but I told my mom everything. She instantly held me and cried with me. It felt like a weight was lifted off my shoulders. I didn't have to carry this alone anymore.

As a young Latina, I understand how our families' experiences and especially being a child of immigrants can affect us greatly. However, I know that I don't have to always take or assume certain beliefs that don't serve me. Not wanting to share our burdens with our families for the fear of not being understood or the fear of being a bother is something perhaps other young Latinas experience too. But that doesn't have to be the case. You matter and you don't have to carry the weight alone.

Thankfully, I began therapy soon after to help me with the trauma I had gone through. While in therapy I was diagnosed with PTSD, anxiety, and depression. I am thankful that I have had support to navigate this journey of healing. I can say that I see the world differently now and am in a better place mentally, emotionally, and physically. The work hasn't been easy, but it has been worth it. My self-esteem and confidence have grown.

While my journey isn't over and I am still continuing therapy today, I am happier and healthier.

When I think about my experience, I see a girl who had to find her inner strength at her weakest moment. I'd like to encourage you to never be afraid to speak up—there is always going to be someone to help you. With whatever you are going through, you are not alone. Therapy is a wonderful tool and I encourage all those who need support to consider it. We are always going through things in our lives, but how we move forward and persevere is what really matters. I have big dreams and I am excited for what the future holds for me. My name is Natalia Ramirez and I am a survivor.

THIS IS ME

I am Natalia Ramirez, a junior attending Dover High School. I currently work at a grocery store on the weekends as a cashier. My family is from Colombia and I am very proud of my heritage. In the future I see myself in a beautiful, well-organized home, with a good salary to help my parents, and traveling around the world with my mother. My mother is my greatest motivator and without her many of my dreams would have come true.

My dream is to be a lawyer specializing in immigration to help those that have stories like me. I would like to help my family come to the United States and I want to give back to my community when I am older. I want to be able to have a voice, and show people that they are not alone. I'd like to be that person that someone can turn to when they need help.

MY TEN-YEAR PLAN:

1. Graduate from law school and join a good law firm.
2. Become a successful, impactful lawyer.
3. Have enough money to give my parents all they need/want.

KEEP TRYING UNTIL YOU MAKE IT

ASHLI ENCARNACION

"Life will put obstacles, but you put limits."
-Anonymous

My life changed dramatically in 2020, but not because of the pandemic. It was actually due to a family matter that had started years before.

In 2016, my mother gave birth to my baby brother. I was 11 years old, so I still remember it very clearly. He was born on a Friday in our hometown of Santo Domingo, in the Dominican Republic. I was the second person to see him—my mother being the first. He was so tiny and so beautiful. From the moment I saw him, I loved him and vowed to be the best big sister ever.

Just before leaving the hospital, my mother noticed a red mark, a spot just above my brother's left eye. The nurses at the hospital said it was probably a scratch or something that happened during delivery and the doctor called it a birthmark, which was not uncommon. Both agreed that the red spot would most likely fade, and they didn't seem concerned, so my mother forgot about it.

Six months later, the mark was not only still there, but it had also begun to swell and grow. My brother's pediatrician diagnosed him with a hemangioma and referred him to a specialist. The new doctor prescribed medicine that stopped the growth, and after a year, it began to shrink. Unfortunately, a year later, the medicine stopped working and the growth returned.

At that point, my mother decided to get a second opinion. Some doctors suggested increasing the prescription amount, while others wanted to try new drugs. This was a problem because the medications were all very expensive and had terrible side effects and risks, yet none of them came with any guarantee that they would work. A couple of the doctors wanted to remove the growth. One surgeon said that he charged a fee of 50,000 pesos and that the hospital, the assistants, and the anesthesiologist would result in additional charges. Another surgeon said that it would be a two-part surgery. He wanted to give my brother, who was three years old at the time, two back-to-back operations with anesthesia. My mother, older brothers, and I began to lose faith that they would ever find my little brother the help that he needed. I was scared for my baby brother and felt like I was letting him down.

I felt helpless and hopeless, but not my mother. She found another doctor. This man listened to everything my brother had been through and looked at my brother's medical history and records. After a careful examination, this doctor said something none of us ever could have expected. He said, "You will not find someone to help this boy here, and if someone says they can, don't trust them. They just want to experiment on your son. I recommend that you start looking outside the country." Then he told my mother what to search for online.

After endless hours of searching, my mother found a doctor who had experience treating children with vascular malformations, the thing the doctor told my mother to research. This doctor was in Manhattan. Determined to get my brother the help he needed, my mother called the hospital, but no one there spoke Spanish and my mother knew very little English. Rather than give up, my mother arranged for a translator. After a long conversation, the doctor agreed to look into my brother's case. After several more phone calls and many months, we traveled to the United States, where they operated on my little brother. Knowing that we had spent almost everything we had to travel to the US, and realizing that we had no insurance, the doctor told my mother that she did not have to pay for the surgery.

After a month in the US, we returned home to the DR. Within a few weeks, my brother forgot about the surgery. Towards the end of 2019, we started noticing signs that my brother's growth was returning. There was some discoloration of his skin and a small bump. In January of 2020, the doctor from the US told my mother that we'd have to return to the US so that he could perform a thorough exam, run tests, and determine if he needed to perform another surgery.

Unfortunately, COVID broke out and due to restrictions and lockdowns, we were unable to travel until August. When my mother informed her employer that she would be taking time off, her boss told her that if she left she would lose her job. My mother decided that her son was more important than any job, so we traveled back to the US.

The second operation was bigger than the previous one. There were more than ten doctors involved, from pediatricians to plastic surgeons. Luckily, everything went well. The doctor wanted my brother to stay in the US for observation and treatment. After thinking about it and talking it over with me, my mother decided to stay here in the US. After all, she didn't have a job to go back to. She had three children to support and my brother's doctor was here. My mother gave me the option of returning to the DR. Although it would be difficult to leave my friends and my home, it would be impossible to leave my mother and little brother alone in the US. I was willing to sacrifice anything for him and for my family.

We spent our year in the US living in one room. I didn't speak any English and didn't know anyone. Because of the COVID restrictions, we couldn't really leave the house, and I had to attend school online. The good news is that my mother was able to find work. I stayed home with my brother who also attended school remotely. He was doing well; the doctors were pleased with the outcome of the second surgery.

The following year, schools opened and I faced a new challenge. I had to leave the tiny room I had become accustomed to being in. On the night before my first day of school, I was nervous. I thought about everything my little brother had been through and how hard my mom worked to make sure he got the help he needed. She was so brave and so strong.

"Mama," I said, "I am scared. I don't know anyone and I don't understand much English. What will I do tomorrow in that big school?"

My mother smiled and said, "Walk in, take a deep breath, and say, 'Hello.'"

By my second year of in-person school, my grades were all A+, and although sometimes I felt out of place, I never stopped trying. I never forgot the strength and determination my mother showed facing challenge after challenge.

Looking back, as I start my last year of high school, I do not regret making the decision to stay in the US. It was difficult, but it was worth it. I will continue to face the rest of my life with the same positive, can-do attitude.

My name is Ashli Enacrancion, and this is the story of how my life changed.

THIS IS ME

My name is Ashli Encarnación, I was born in the Dominican Republic. I live with my family in New Jersey in a small town, Dover. I am a senior in high school. I am very involved in school things, like the dance club, Latin mix club (it's a Latin dance club), interact club, peer mentor (help other students), fundraisers, and my prom party. Dancing and helping others are my favorite hobbies. I also work after school and help take care of my little brother.

My lifelong dream has been to become a doctor. I always wanted to be that doctor who saved someone. Since I was a child, I always said that I wanted to study medicine. Although as the years passed and I matured, I realized that studying medicine is very expensive. That's why I'm saving a lot to fulfill my dream.

MY TEN-YEAR PLAN:

1. Get my nursing degree.
2. Get a Pediatric Nursing Degree.
3. Work to help people.

A BUNDLE OF SENTIMENTS

CAROLINA SUERO

"Nevertheless, she persisted."

My first memories are in the place I used to call home. The place where the flowers are vibrant and the trees were so tall they touched the sky. The place where I learned how to speak, walk, and live. The place where I, unfortunately, found out that when people pass away, they go to the sky—only to make me paranoid that the sky would fall due to overcapacity.

The memory goes like this: I am outside La Casa Grande, where my grandma lives, and I am with my cousin. She somehow convinced me that she was the reason my great-grandpa died and told me that the wind blowing was him screaming at her through the heavens. It did not help that I was about three years old—my consciousness was just developing! That night I lay in bed and looked at the stars through the hole in my roof. I begged the heavens to forgive my poor cousin, she didn't mean to do it. At least, I think that is how it went; I was only three.

From my earliest memory in my favorite home, I have

somehow always been an anxious person. You could imagine what it was like the day I had to leave my home. From what I recall, I did not open my eyes. My family begged me to look, but I thought maybe if I kept them closed, it wouldn't be a reality. In my head, I could still curl up with my abuelita and let her sing to me. I could still go to my pre-k and scream whenever I saw a spider on my desk. But I couldn't, and I knew that, so I closed my eyes. I didn't say goodbye.

It was December 11, 2009, and I was in the clouds. The heavens were right outside my window and I could tell my grandpa must love it up there. Our flight was 45 minutes long. Ninety miles, yet I landed in a completely different world, Miami. I knew there was this place outside of my home that was beautiful and big—it was so imposing. Leaving the plane, I would think to myself that I was in a movie. The long walk down the immigration line was my runway (instrumental music played in the background). I looked up at my mom, who told me, "This is home now," which brought me back. I knew this couldn't be a movie nor a dream.

A NEW LIFE

Just like that, life moved on from my past. It left the trees and the flowers and the skies. The world I now lived in was new, which was unexplainably difficult to get used to. "The land of opportunity" was not something I took for granted, though it took me some time to get there.

Miami is a big mumbo jumbo of ethnicities, and my little

corner of the jumbo was where all the Cubans were. The culture was the most prevalent thing about our city; Cuba was in the local businesses, the schools, and the streets. The transition was seamless. English came quickly to me, and I got put into the gifted program at my elementary school.

Life was great, but then came the divorce. Like most, it was messy. More than anything, it was an eye-opening experience. I went from having the luxury of ignorance, in regards to my family, to suddenly being thrown in this whirlpool of emotions.

For my mom, I had to be resilient. The suffering of my family would not be a subject of my own; if anything, I would be at their disposal for whatever they needed. I now have a better understanding of what my mom was going through, but back then I did my best with the bit of maturity I had. She would now be a single mother who would have to figure out a way to support my brother and I. She was—and is—superwoman to me.

As time passed, I started noticing the discrepancies in our community toward women. This pedestal I had my mother on was not a shared thought. People saw her as weak for giving up on her marriage. How could they think that when she was the absolute opposite? I just saw her as someone who always found a way to take me to school and put food on my table. I always knew that there was this strange relationship between how women are treated vs. how men are, but I never truly saw the light of day on this till I had to confront it myself.

THE UNFORSAKEN DAY

I got my period on October 1, 2016, and it had to be the worst day of my life. One: I did not know what a period was. Two: I stained pants and had no pads on me. I could've cursed the world with my distress. What was I going to do? How was I ever going to live this down? The thoughts were sprinkled confetti in my head, and I went blank. My anxiousness was always creeping up, but in this situation it outright slammed me in my face.

When I went back to my classroom to receive heinous comments from immature classmates, I felt so inferior. The resilience suddenly vanished, and I wanted to transport back to the clouds and the place I used to call home.

But I couldn't. My mother, my family, and every woman before me did not defy odds just for me to go ahead and let something as silly as ignorance destroy all of the progress I made since my parents divorced the year prior to this. With time, I recollected enough strength and courage to do something about it.

The Hygiene Project, INC. came to be, which provides free, hygienic products to public school students. This was done so that no one would have to glimpse what I felt that day. They would always have products at their disposal. It also gives students this feeling of belonging, as though someone else is looking out for them, even if it is not directly. It gives them a sense of home. After years of continuously seeing women lack resources and overall respect, I knew this project would be a breath of fresh air.

This project is the opposite of who my younger self was. It

requires me to put aside my fears and vocalize what I care about. I'm required to facilitate conversations and give others a platform to showcase their activism. I learned that if I based my success on what others thought of me and let those sentiments win, I would have made my immigrant journey pointless. Our potential as Latinx women is ever-growing and, though we have to learn to push through the bitterness, we are still pretty awesome.

I am a bundle of sentiments shaped from my past and created for my future. You and I are identical, except we are made up of different components. So, since we are one and the same, take it from me and never throw away a passion just because life may lead you to give up. Never feel bound to one specific place that gives you comfort. Nevertheless, persist.

THIS IS ME

My name is Carolina Suero, and I am a senior at Jose Marti MAST 6-12 Academy. I am a part-time swim instructor and a full-time executive director for my nonprofit, The Hygiene Project.

In the future, I hope to continue my work in advocacy, specifically for Latinx menstruators. Along with this, I am also pursuing a career in law, where I would love to dabble in politics and the federal government!

MY TEN-YEAR PLAN:

1. Study abroad with Semester at Sea and overcome my fear of the ocean! (This is also so I can eat a bunch of cool food from different countries.)

2. Get my law degree and use it to help legitimize my activism more.

3. Create and be a part of more organizations to help combat different social issues that I partake in.

GUERRERA REINA

ITTATY AGUILAR-GUZMAN

"And always remember this, the world is going to judge you no matter what, so live life the way you want to."

Dreams built from sacrifices, sweat, tears, and hearts looking forward to better days to create a legacy. My parents' lives are split between two lands and I becoming the first to bridge such a gap is no easy task. It takes a lot of discipline, ambition, courage, humbleness, and a heart of gold. Even the toughest warrior cries, but that is okay because we are human, and it is normal to have emotions. My family and contributing to this world are my driving force. Every day I have the same grit that keeps me going despite challenges arising, but rarely is there a second type of event. The kind I never want to have, that comes without warning and that knocks me down expecting me to give up.

For as long as I can remember, I was always the odd one from the crowd. I always wanted to be different and for that I was always faced with many challenges. Growing up, I've been bullied by my own peers, professors, and even individuals I knew and trusted. Despite coming home from difficult days, internally crying, I always had and continue to have my dedicated support system at home—my mother with her comfort and homemade meals that made me feel invincible and my father, a hardworking man, that I can get advice and wisdom from like a crystal ball. Although he may not have the solutions, he is a great teacher. I also can't forget my younger siblings, for they are my anchor, too.

I would always ask and hear about my parents' past, what they went through growing up and the sacrifices they made. It fueled the internal fire to keep fighting and continuing to achieve not just my dreams, but my parents' dreams.

I also questioned my roots, who I am and if I was ever enough. In high school, I was never the popular one and avoided any drama. I was viewed as a ghost, the forgotten one and, by many, a nobody with no future. I was bullied for the oddest reasons, such as going to technical school, for my opinions, for the bully's manifestation of social status and their own pleasure. I knew that if I told on the system, nothing and no adequate actions would be taken because the ones at fault would be either be on class student boards, sports varsity teams, or have parents on the academic boards or be fundraising parents for the school system.

I thought I could just run away from problems, and so I attended a technical school/advance academy to have a head start in higher education and have a fresh start, but I was wrong. The same challenges arose and followed, but with time I learned to mask the emotional and psychological damage that had been done as before. I never really knew what mental health was nor was it ever talked about. I found myself enclosing in my own ideas and thoughts, becoming a cold person and not really caring about others.

I would always find myself asking, "Ma, Pa, porque el mal existe y porque la gente me tratan mal?" *(Ma, Pa, why does bad exist, and why do people treat me bad?)*

I would be reminded, "Challenges, bad people, come onto our paths, because one is an untamable mustang, a warrior, and capable of handling anything. And always remember this, the world is going to judge you no matter what, so live life the way you want to."

During my first year of college, I was nervous and scared, but excited to take a step into the real world with a fresh start. I knew it was going to be difficult and challenging, as the first-generation student to experience such a big change. To take on a STEM career, or any career, is very challenging, as there are pressures from every angle to be the perfect student.

During my spring break in 2017, I went to Mexico on a study abroad trip and this opened my eyes. I finally felt whole and could see where my roots were from and how fortunate I was to have this life changing opportunity. I returned from the trip full of new inspiration to keep going in achieving my goals.

During my years as an undergrad, I started to get burnt out frequently, and continue to ignore my mental health. It took a turn for the worse when the academic courses became more difficult. I started to feel high levels of anxiety. I felt lost, out of place, and lonesome. My academic performance tanked and I finally cracked. I was embarrassed and ashamed to admit to my advisors that I needed help in taking my mental health seriously, but with their guidance and assurance I did seek adequate help and still use it to this day.

From then on, I thought the only challenge I had to overcome was the stigma of being a perfect student and trying to get into medical school. I started to close myself off and try to hide it behind a smile. Once again, I had the endurance to keep going. I'm still here, moving through life to achieve my goals, one step at a time, one challenge at a time.

THIS IS ME

Born and raised in Wyoming, MI, a suburb of Grand Rapids, I am a first-generation college graduate and the eldest of eight children. I am proud to be the daughter of immigrant parents—my father, an entrepreneur, and mother a stay-home supporter. My higher education started early on while in high school, I began with my interests in medicine, law, and entrepreneurship. I graduated with Biomedical Laboratory Sciences concentration in Medical Microbiology and Human Biology on a Pre-Medical track from Michigan State University.

Currently, I am completing the Masters in Global Health at Michigan State University and will progress further into higher education. I aspire to attend medical school to become a medical officer in the United States Armed Forces, to travel and serve internationally. I have traveled abroad to serve communities such as remodeling schools, educating kids, and motivating the younger generation. I have devoted my life to learning, teaching, and servicing locally, nationally, and globally.

In my free time I enjoy traveling, doing equine activities, and making art. I would love to extend my gratitude to thank my family, friends, mentors, instructors, and advisors for my success. I am committed to giving back in the future to help others succeed in academics and serving the nation.

MY TEN-YEAR PLAN:

1. Attend professional schools; medical/law school

2. Travel the world to serve

3. Mentor the younger generation

DEJHANAYRA ARGUETA

"This is just the beginning and it's only going to get better from here"

What do you want to be when you grow up? That is the timeless question that all kids and teens are asked. An honest question, but what I personally have had to discover is, *How* do I decide what I want to be?

As a current senior in high school, I am always asked these types of questions about what colleges I plan to apply to, what major do I plan to choose, and what career do I want to pursue. In the beginning of my freshman year, my answer to most of these questions was unknown. It was impossible to have an answer as I began high school the year the pandemic began. With the isolation and untypical school scenario, it was a challenge trying to discover myself, when the whole world was on pause. This uncertainty, lead me to set a goal to uncover who I was by my junior year and determine what I want to be at the end of my senior year.

Freshman year, I was on the cheer team, living life cheering at football, basketball games, and I was a band student. My young life was going well. However, in March 2020, the entire world shut down, and I did as well. All the commotion of the pandemic transferred into my life it seemed like. I developed a knee injury during that time that prevented me from trying out for the cheer team that untimely lead me to not making the team my sophomore year. It took a toll on me because most of my friends who were on the team cut me out of their lives. I felt alone, which made me feel unmotivated and I let my grades and self-esteem drop. I was so angry with the world and at everyone as they continued with life, meanwhile I was just sitting there on pause. My two older sisters are quite accomplished so I would often compare myself and felt disappointed I was going through this phase.

Thankfully, my sisters and parents recognized the pain I was in and they began to help me. They were my wakeup call and they encouraged me to get involved in other activities. I got involved in Yearbook, Softball and FCCLA (Family, Career and Community Leaders of America). Most of my self-improvement was because of FCCLA. I am so thankful for this organization and all the amazing things that changed in my life because of it. FCCLA was run by two amazing teachers who were also my advisors. Their impact was so profound, I cannot possibly describe how it changed me inside and out. It allowed me to step outside my comfort zone and I did things like run for an officer position, apply to my first paid job, and get hired as marketing manager! From then on, I learned it is okay to take a chance and jump!

You never know what is on the other side. FCCLA allowed me to also compete under the Leadership event to which I made it to the State Finals and then Nationals in June 2022 in San Diego, California. I was presented with a medal in front of my family which had a significant meaning to me. In that moment I was empowered and determined to do more great things. Everything I had learned through FCCLA taught me to grow as a better leader, create a better version of myself and be willing to help others create their own story/journey too. The leadership skills I developed like growing my communication, personal and technical skills allow me to connect and help others find their own way like I once did.

Of course, at times it is inevitable to feel like an impostor. I definitely battled through this and felt like I didn't deserve the success and accomplishments I had. But what I found in the middle of this was that when I help people, that impostor syndrome leaves. I realized that helping others felt so natural and that it made me think was in fact discovering my purpose in this world. Ironically, these skills I learned came in handy at the right time. Through a course I am taking, I had the opportunity to become a Certified Nursing Assistant and work at a nursing home helping residents. I grew to understand the pain the residents go through, and what I can do in order to help them. I was able to see firsthand how some of the residents feel unless or felt like burden. I made it my mission to truly care for all my patients and connect with them. I wanted to be there for them and make a positive change in their lives.

As I was experiencing this opportunity, the answer to the timeless question I had asked myself reveled itself to me. I decided I wanted to purse a career in healthcare and become a doctor. I was exposed to real struggles inside that healthcare facility. How some providers and staff had the wrong motivations to help, seeking money first, mistreating patients, not providing the emotional support our patients or their families needed, etc. I also thought of my sister Yahayra, who had gone through a malpractice situation that has affected her life, when she dislocated her hip at age 11 and had two surgeries performed incorrectly. Or even myself, with my own injury where I felt unheard by my medical team. I know what it's like to not feel understood when you're going through pain and feel like the doctor is just treating your symptom and no YOU. I want to be part of those great doctor patient relationships and I do take these details into consideration, even now as I work in my smaller capacity. My desire is to be able to help lower malpractice cases, stop the mistreatment patient receives, and be able to assure families they are in good hands.

I am looking forward to the future and continuing to help those in need. I can't wait to learn more and dedicate myself to helping patients grow stronger day by day. If I am lucky enough, I would love to be involved in malpractices cases to help families find peace in the pain and struggle. I know the journey won't be easy but I am willing to work hard and persevere. I encourage you to also find opportunities and take a jump like I once did. That is what life is about, improving yourself and finding your purpose to serve and help others. I am not just a young Latina with a dream, I am someone who was born with a special purpose to share with the world. There is a long list to follow with many options, many walls and barriers in my journey but I am ready to knock them down. Following through with my plan is not an option, it's a promise I am ready to fulfill.

THIS IS ME:

My name is Dejhanayra Argueta, I am currently 17 years old from Aurora, IL, a west suburb of Chicago. I am the youngest of three daughters and I am currently a Senior at West Aurora High School. My family is from Mexico and I am very proud of my heritage. I am currently applying to different colleges and will pursuing the pre-med track. I have been involved in FCCLA, a great program through that has helped me develop my leadership skills. I speak three languages and in the process of earning my seal by literacy in French, Spanish and English. My dream is to graduate Medical School and receive my white coat in front of my entire family. Earning my coat would not just be an achievement for me but an honor of becoming the person I was born to be. My goal is to help others live a better life and being trilingual will help me work with many people and be involved in numerous medical cases. This will help give me an advantage to one day improve the healthcare system and with enough hard work, I hope to earn a leading role as a Medical Director in my future.

MY TEN-YEAR PLAN:

1. Complete college in the pre-med track
2. Graduate Medical School and receiving my white coat in front of my family
3. Work in Hospital and become a Medical Director

About the Authors

JACQUELINE S. RUIZ

BIOGRAPHY

Jacqueline Ruiz is a visionary social entrepreneur that has created an enterprise of inspiration. With more than 20 years of experience in the Marketing and Public Relations industry, she has created two successful award-winning companies, established two nonprofit organizations, published 29 books, including the largest collection of Latina stories in a book anthology series in the world, and has held events in four continents.

She has received over 30 awards for her contributions and business acumen. Jacqueline speaks to hundreds of audiences about marketing, servant leadership, finding your passion, and achieving success in business. She has addressed the United States Army, Airbus, BP International, United Airlines, Allstate, Northern Trust US + Europe and Farmers Insurance among other corporations to share her inspiration. She has been featured in Forbes, INC Magazine, Univision, Telemundo, ABC 7, NBC 5, among others.

She is one of the few Latina sports airplane pilots in the United States.

About the Authors

ALEXANDRIA RIOS TAYLOR

BIOGRAPHY

Alexandria Rios Taylor is a high school Principal at Mundelein High School located in the northern suburbs of Chicago. She was recently appointed to the Illinois School Board of Education's School Health Advisory Committee where she advises the State Board of Education on all matters relating to the implementation of the provisions of the Critical Health Problems and Comprehensive Health Education Act. She also assists in establishing a sound understanding and sympathetic relationship between such comprehensive health education programs and the public health, welfare and educational programs of other agencies in the community.

Prior to the Principalship, she served as Assistant Principal of Student Services at Glenbard East High school in Lombard, IL, and Dean of Students at Glenbard West High School. She served as Equity Coordinator in Glenbard District 87 and mentored youth on leadership development and academic success.

Aside from education, Alexandria has partnered with Jaqueline Camacho Ruiz on the *Today's Inspired Young Latina* series. They are publishing volume IV in December of 2022 and have given over 65 young students and young professionals the ability to narrate their stories, define their pathway and become published authors.

Alexandria is currently pursuing her doctorate degree in educational administration at Aurora University as she examines the pipeline of Latina Leadership. She holds a master's degree in leadership and administration from Benedictine University and completed her undergraduate studies at North Central College. She double majored and earned a bachelor's degree in both organizational communication and Spanish where she received the Carleen Verstraete Award and the Rasmussen Scholarship. Alex was later recognized by her alma mater and received the Sesquicentennial Award in education as a top educator in her decade and the Outstanding Alumnus Award in 2020.

Alexandria delivers addresses and presentations drawing upon her personal experience in public education as well as integrating data from her doctoral research. Her research about Latina leadership has served as the foundation for conference sessions, workshops, and content development.

Although she is proud of her tenure as an educator and service to her community, nothing gives Alex more gratification than coming home to her two kids, Elena and Maceo, and her devoted husband, Gentri.

Made in the USA
Columbia, SC
05 December 2022